THE PO[illegible] *Of Simple* OBEDIENCE

By

PASTOR RAMSON B. MUMBA JR.

Published By:
Get Understanding Publishing
Restoration House
Bradford, England

If you would like more information about this ministry or are interested in becoming a covenant partner, please write:

Centre Of Life Church International
Restoration House
Nelson Street
Bradford,
England
BD5 0HD
Tel: +44 (0) 1274 724557
Website: www.centreoflife.org
Email: information@centreoflife.org

Unless otherwise indicated, all Scripture quotations are taken from the King James Version of the Bible.

ISBN 1-904066-00-3

Cover Design By Adeola Disu

Printed By: Printpoint, Bradford. 01274 575696

To all those who are willing to do whatever it takes to obey God.

This book is dedicated to all the faithful members and partners of the Centre Of Life Church International, whose hunger for the uncompromised Word of God has inspired me to keep reaching to God for fresh revelation and insight. It is indeed a joy, an honour and a pleasure to pastor such a great people. El Shaddai Dome is on its way.

Many thanks also to my lovely wife, Linda, for releasing me to write this book and supporting me throughout the project with all her wise counsel. You are indeed a sweetheart.

I am indebted to my wonderful team of staff for all the effort expended on this book, especially to Judith Hopkins and Clare Kirton, my Personal Assistant, for proofreading the material.

Table Of Contents

Chapter One

Introduction - A Question Of Balance

The subject of obedience to God can easily be turned into legalistic teaching that subtly robs people of the grace of God that is now freely available to all New Testament believers. One has to admit though that obedience is rather strong meat, which most believers are unable to digest by failing to rightly divide the Word of truth. Consequently we need to bring balance to the subject right at the outset. Balance, however, is neither rebellion nor a licence to sin. The scripture says that *'the grace of God that brings salvation has appeared to all men. It teaches us to say "No" to ungodliness and worldly passions and to live self-controlled, upright and godly lives in this present age,* ***Titus 2: 11 - 13.*** As an individualistic society, riddled with independent spirits, that frequently resents any talk of submission and respect for authority, the message of obedience is bound to be unpopular. However, because of the power that is inherent in simple obedience, we have to tackle the subject if we are to live in the full manifestation of our covenant rights and privileges with God.

Every world economic system has its system of exchange. Even before money was invented, they had what they called a barter system in which people were exchanging goods for goods. Then people started trading in gold, which over the subsequent years evolved into money. In most countries today, money is the medium of exchange. Today in almost any economic system of exchange, if you haven't got any money, you cannot legally obtain your desired goods and services. As matter of fact, most people don't care how hungry you are, if you cannot make the proper exchange in order to receive the benefit of their goods and services. They might be mean, but that's just the way it is. Likewise in the Kingdom of God system, obedience is the medium of exchange, or the currency in which you deal. Without obedience, you will fail to legally receive the full benefits of the covenant.

The Kingdom of God works by established principles or spiritual laws. A principle is an established law. That means these principles will work for anybody who will dare to put them to work. They work even if you perceive that they are not working. These principles work for educated people; they work for illiterate people; they work for tall folk and they work for short folk. They work for black folk. They work for white folk. They work for red folk. They work for yellow folk. Basically, principles will yield results for anybody who will apply them effectively. God has decreed that, 'If you want my principle of blessing by exchange to work for you, put it to work. God is no respecter of persons, but He is a respecter of faith or principle.

Therefore, every time something is not working, it isn't God who is at fault. God is not going to establish another covenant; He's not going to send Jesus back to the cross just so He can add to this last Testament whatever it is that you desire. Either this covenant works or Jesus was not telling the truth when He announced to the Jews that, *'heaven and earth shall pass away, but not one tittle, or one iota of His Word shall pass away.'* In other words, this covenant is forever settled in Heaven.

In spite of such sobering truths, most people still spend all their lives wishing God would change His system of operating just to suit how they would like things to be done. They say, 'oh, if God really loves me, He should have changed the system just for me'. Well big deal, sitting at home thinking about how God should design such spiritual laws to accommodate your wishes is going help you a whole lot! That's like a man looking at food and saying, 'I wish God had just created it so that when I look at food I could be satisfied, because I cannot be bothered to get up and eat.' That will not change a thing.

Deuteronomy 11: 26 - 28 says, *'Behold I set before you a blessing and a curse; a blessing if you obey the commandments of the Lord your God, which I command you this day; And a curse if you will not obey the commandments of the Lord your God, but turn aside out of the way which I command you this day to go after other gods, which you have not known'.* God has not left any of us to have our lives run by chance. He has given us established and tested principles to live by so that we may walk in the fullness of His grace that is ours through Jesus Christ.

In the book of **Isaiah 1: 19**, God said, *"If you are willing and obedient, you will eat the good of the land"*. Like it was in the time of the Prophet Isaiah, Judah was a rebellious Nation, which had substituted the fear of the Lord and obedience for ritual and sacrifices, so it is in our own day. Yes, people go to church. Some even bring tithes and offerings, while others go even a step further by keeping all the five feasts according to the book of the Law, but still the Lord is not pleased with them. They all talk about the covenant promises that they have with God but in reality very few of them have seen the full manifestation of these covenantal promises.

The truth is that God has no problem with you eating the good of the land. He is inexhaustible. You couldn't eat all He has got. You can get all you want to, but there will still be plenty left over. He is El Shaddai, the God who is more than enough. So He is not holding out on you and He is not your problem. The sticking point is that God's spiritual law is a system working only by exchange. Therefore, for any one to jump into the 'eating the good of the land' part of that scripture without willingly obeying God is to pervert spiritual law. None of us have a right to withdraw from where we have not made any deposits. Consequently, obedience is the biggest key to releasing all of God's ability in your life.

Chapter Two

The Law Of Blessing By Exchange

Every system of exchange has a currency in which you deal. In the *Kingdom of God* system you deal with God based on your obedience. Obedience is the medium of exchange for your goods and services in the "Kingdom of God" system. Imagine that you went to a grocery store and took some items of interest. When you got to the checkout, what would you have to give in exchange for those items? Imagine also that you absolutely refused to produce money in exchange for the items. Would you legally walk out with those items? I suspect that chances are that you would either have to put the items back on the shelves or be arrested for attempted robbery. The reason for all this would not be because the management of the grocery store are mean. It is simply because you had not made the proper exchange for those items.

Most Christians do not want to make the proper exchange for what they desire to receive from God. After all, Jesus died and the blessing must be free. That is not true. It is going to cost obedience. The love of God is unconditional, but most, if not all, of God's promises are conditional. Obedience is the currency of exchange. Therefore, obedience is the key to the *Kingdom of God* system. If you are going to factor into God's way of doing things, you have to learn to simply obey. When you obey God, you can have all that He has. God always works by laws. The whole *Kingdom of God* system is based on this way of operating. Obedience is the law that governs the *Kingdom of God* system.

When I was a Business Student learning economics, one of the concepts that we were taught was what they called *'the opportunity cost.'* Simply stated, the opportunity cost of something reflects the true value of what a person exchanges in order to obtain it. For instance, the true cost of attending a church meeting is not so much, how much fuel it is going to cost you to drive the distance. The true cost includes the fuel cost, the wear and tear on the car, what you could not do because you are at church - that television programme you are not watching because you are not at home, and many more other alternative options you have forfeited. That is the true cost of coming to church. So it is a much bigger cost. However, the value of obeying the commandment to *'forsake not the assembling together'* far outweighs the cost of the exchange. The bottom line with obedience is what value you place on the exchange at stake. The whole system is therefore dependent on how desperate you are and whether or not you place a premium on seeing the predestined plan of God for your life come to pass.

Your lot in life is considerably, if not predominantly, determined by your obedience. Willingness and obedience are keys to eating the good of the land. The problem however, is that most Christians think that they can consistently eat the good of the land without paying the price of obedience. Many want God's blessing on the cheap. Countless thousands want the Will of God for their lives realised without paying the price called obedience. The trouble is that God's love is free, but all the promises of God depend on obedience.

Deuteronomy 11: 26 - 28. *Behold, I set before you today, a blessing and a curse; the blessing if you obey the commandments of the Lord your God which I command you today; and the curse, if you do not obey the commandments of the Lord your God, but turn aside from the way which I command you today, to go after other gods which you have not known.*

The word blessing is a covenant word, which means empowerment to prosper. To prosper is to have sufficiency in every area of your human existence. To come up from anything that has held you back and kept you down and under. What Moses is saying is, look this isn't too hard, I have set before you this empowerment, this ability, this anointing to prosper which is the blessing if you walk in obedience. This is the key - if you obey it's a blessing.

If you disobey, however, it is a curse. It is an empowerment to fail. I mean just licensed to fail. Have you ever wondered why some people are always failing? Their finances never working right, no soundness in their mind? They sit and wonder whether or not God has abandoned them. The truth is, He hasn't. He has already set it all before you. The whole deal is on the table. Success and failure; blessing and curses; sickness and healing; deliverance and bondage; freedom and fear; a sound mind, everything that makes for your highest good is on the table, and everything that will and can empower you to fail, is on the table too. Will you walk home with the goodies or will you keep mickey-mousing about and then keep blaming it on God?

In its simplicity, wanting to obey God is willing to go home with a sound mind, with a sound marriage, with a sound bank account, with a sound household and everything that He promised to do for you in the Bible. That is what the exchange is for. It's not what God is getting. For example, when you give your tithe, it's not the money that moves God to open the windows of heaven and rebuke the devourer on your behalf. There is no Bank of Heaven where they deposit currency notes. It is the obedience that is behind your money that you exchange, that rebukes the devourer and opens the windows of heaven in your life for blessing.

The reason you feel bound by unforgiveness, is not so much what they did to you or what you would have to sacrifice in order to forgive and move on. The decision to forgive is not the exchange. The obedience is the exchange, and it releases you from what they did to you. The choice is yours. You can choose to disregard the covenant to the point where you end up in hell, even though God has already prepared heaven for you. In His kindness, though, God has also made some recommendations for you and me.

Deuteronomy 30: 19 - 20. *I call heaven and earth as witnesses today against you, that I have set before you life and death, blessing and cursing; therefore choose life, that both you and your descendants may live; that you may love the Lord your God, that you may obey His voice, that you may cling to Him, for He is your life and the length of your days; that you may dwell in the land which the Lord swore to your fathers, to Abraham, Isaac and Jacob, to give them.*

God makes a recommendation as to what He knows is good for you. Therefore, from now on, settle it forever. God is not the author of your trouble. God has set it all out before you. The choice is yours. Choose to walk in love. Choose the blessing. Choose forgiveness. Choose to pray for those that despitefully use you. Choose a meek and gentle and quiet spirit. Choose to do what's right and only because it's right. Choose obedience that both you and your children may live the God-kind of abundant life.

It is also extremely important to understand that God operates by covenant. A covenant is an agreement between two or more parties to carry out the terms of that agreement. The covenant is a two-sided deal. It has a blessing for keeping it and it carries a curse for breaking it. It is important to note, however, that God sets the terms of the covenant. When you come to God, it's either on His terms or no terms. Most believers do not like that. The world literally detests this. They retort, 'who does God think He is? Well, He actually believes that He is God. He actually believes He's the Almighty God. He actually believes He's the creator of the Heavens and the Earth. He actually believes that he brings the counsel of nations to nothing.

In the light of the covenant, the way God always operates is that He first of all gives a promise. ***Amos 3: 7*** says, *'surely the Sovereign Lord does nothing unless He reveals His secret to His servants the prophets.'* God never does anything without first making a promise through the mouth of His prophets. Even with regard to redemption, God had to make a promise first. Then with God, it's His terms or no terms at all. Most Christians go about making their own plans, and then ask God to bless the plans. The truth is that God is not obligated to bless anything that is not born out of Him. He may bless your plans out of His mercy and He does. The best way is to just get His plans, they are already blessed because God is obligated to bless His own plans and see to it that they succeed.

Without making any exchange, there can be no cutting of covenant. However, there are a lot of Christians who come to the altar without bringing the exchange of obedience. They want to cut the covenant on the cheap. They haven't sacrificed anything. They wonder why God isn't blessing them. The terms are obedience in exchange for anything that He has already promised us already in the Word. It is His terms or no terms at all.

I always wondered why in the Old Testament, every time, anybody went near to where God was, they took a sacrifice, an offering. They couldn't even see the prophet without an offering. Remember when Saul lost his donkeys. Saul's aide said to him, 'there is a prophet in the town. Let's go and see him.' Saul's reply was, *'I cannot go, I haven't got a sacrifice or an offering for the man of God'*. The reason was that the Old Testament saints understood that you'd have to make an exchange in order to factor in the covenant. Therefore, God first of all makes the promise. He sets it all out on the table. If you obey Him, you know exactly what to expect. It's called the blessing. If you disobey Him, you know exactly what to expect. It's called the curse.

Both the blessing and the curse come from God. The devil cannot bless you neither can he curse you. He has not got the authority to do that because there is no truth in him. Do you remember when Balak hired Balaam to come and curse the nation of Israel because he didn't feel too good that God was with them? Balaam tried to curse them, and the Spirit of the Lord kept saying, no, you cannot curse what I have blessed. In other words, it does not matter how much the devil hates you. If God has blessed you, you are untouchable. If you obey God, you always abide under the shadow of the Almighty, and you can always say that the Lord is your refuge and your strength.

Further, there are certain spiritual laws that even God Himself cannot violate; your free will being one of them.

Now, obedience legally allows God to bless you. It is illegal for God to do certain things. I know we believe God can do everything, but that is not completely true. For instance, God cannot get born again for you however much He loves you. You have to confess Jesus with your mouth as Lord, and believe in your heart that God raised Him from the dead. Same thing, if you do not keep the book of the law in you mouth and meditate on it day and night, that you may observe to do according to what is written therein, you will not make your way prosperous and have good success. Obedience gives God the legal right to step into your life.

You are a free moral agent. God cannot override your will. If you do not yield your will to Him, God is paralysed in your life. There are multitudes of people who have in their midst the answers to all the problems for their lives, but they have paralysed that answer. This is because every time God gives them words, they say that they know better than God's counsel. They have become smarter than God. If you have an excuse for everything, it is evidence of the fact that you are unteachable. In other words, you do not want to change. Change is only change when you have changed. Talking about it doesn't make it change. By the same token, obedience is not obedience until you obey or act in line with the command in question.

Obedience has to become the most natural thing that you do. It just becomes second nature. Remember at the wedding in Cana in Galilee what Mary told those servants, *'whatever He tells you to do, just do it.'* Whatever He tells you to do. It doesn't matter what it looks like.

It doesn't matter if it is costing you something. Yes, it is a sacrifice. But simple obedience is the most powerful weapon in your entire arsenal as a Christian. Consider the following promises of God.

Deuteronomy 7: 12 - 15 & 21. *'if you pay attention to these laws and carefully follow them, then the Lord your God will keep His covenant of love with you, as he swore to your forefathers. He will love you and bless you, and increase your number. He will bless the fruit of your womb, the crop of your land, the grain, your new wine and oil, the calves of your herd, and the lambs of your flocks in the land that He swore to your forefathers to give you. You will be blessed more than any other peoples. None of your men or women will be childless, or any of your livestock without young. The Lord will keep you free from every disease. He will not inflict on you the horrible diseases you knew in Egypt, but He will inflict them on all who hate you.' 'Do not be terrified by them, for the Lord your God, who is among you, is a great and awesome God'.*

What Moses was saying to the children of Israel was; if you hate God by disobeying Him, then you have chosen the curse. Sickness and disease is already under the curse, so you just receive the whole deal. But, just the simplicity of whatsoever he tells you to do, just do it, carries power with it. Power is the ability to cause change and in obedience it makes you get power, or a position, where you can get some things changed, because you obeyed God.

The question you should be asking is, 'Does my will line up with the word of God?' It doesn't matter - it's just like righteousness

- righteousness is not based on what is accepted in society. Righteousness is doing what God said to do about your situation. But if you think righteousness or obedience is based on what is popular, then you are going to miss God's standard of perfection. So, when I talk about obedience, I'm not talking about the fact that you are not in trouble. When I talk about obedience, I'm not only talking about you committing sins of commission but also sins of omission. Sometimes, you can miss God, not so much by what you do, but sometimes by what you do not do. *Just like to him that knows how to do good, but does not do good, to him it is a sin.* It doesn't mean that you necessarily committed sin by your outward action, but that you did not act or do something when it was within your power to do so.

Unless we begin to be willing and obedient, we will always be children. We will always be immature and as the Apostle Paul said to the Corinthians, 'I couldn't talk to you as spiritual because you were still carnal, you were still immature, you were still acting like children, fighting over who you belonged to. In other words, God cannot give you the depth of revelation because you are not yet mature enough to handle it. It is all based on the fact that you are not willing to yield your will. This is a Covenant, a blood-sworn Oath, where God can never change His mind if you take Him at His Word. The Bible doesn't contain the Word of God. It is the Word of God. Whatever God can do, His Word can do. That's why man shall not live by bread alone, but by every Word that proceeds from the mouth of God. The Word of God was not given so we could have intellectual debates about it; it was given so that as we obey it, we might live the God kind of abundant life.

Chapter Three

Hallmarks Of Authentic Obedience

The Lord spoke to me once saying, *'there are many Christians who have accepted Him as their Saviour, but there are very few who have accepted Him as Lord in every area of their lives.'* Many Christians know God as Saviour. They love to hear messages about being those who are saved, delivered, provided for, healed, set free, and brought into their abundance. But when God comes down to talk to them as Lord, it becomes a whole different ball game. They claim to be a post-modernistic society. Most people nowadays are too deep, examining everything and not willing to take God at His Word. They have ceased to be believers only - Now they are debaters and doubters. If it doesn't suit them too well, they reason that maybe it's not really saying what it is saying. They then start to look for a paraphrase or another translation.

Who is this God that we have come to believe in? Have we created our own God, who we can tell what to do, when He can do it and how He can do it? The God we serve is God all by Himself. And Jesus declared in ***John 5: 26***, a very simple, yet profound statement; *'The Father has life in Himself.'* Meaning, all of life stems from the Father. He is the giver of all things, and yet He does not need anybody to give it to Him. Even if we were all to become atheist, it would still neither add nor subtract anything from who He is. He is God all by Himself, who only shares His glory with those who are willing to obey Him in righteousness. Right standing with God does not make Him your peer. He's Almighty God. He alone is the only Most High God. Out of covenant, God relates to those who obey Him as friend, but He is still to be feared. He is the Most High God. God is an Almighty God. Greatly to be feared above all gods.

The Bible declares in the book of ***Revelation 4: 11*** *that, God has created all things and for His pleasure they are created.* Further, in the book of ***Colossians 1: 15 - 17***, it says that, *'all things were made by Him and for Him and in Him all things consist.'* In other words, God exists for Himself, but yet out of His own goodness has allowed us to partake in His divine nature. Therefore, when it comes to dealing with God, He does not do deals on any other terms but His. It is either God's terms or no terms at all.

Just a consideration of the lives of all the Bible characters thoroughly illustrates this truth. Joshua in particular discovered this truth when he said to the Angel of the Lord, *'Are you for us, or for our adversary?'* The Angel answered him and said, 'Neither'. Meaning, I'm not for you boys and I'm not for those boys. I'm not for your enemies and I'm not for you. I'm for myself.' Now whose side are you on? I'm on my own side. Now which side are you on?' God is on his own side. The choice is whose side are you going to be on.

What then is the picture that the Bible paints when it refers to us obeying God? The picture is that of rank and order. Rank of importance, authority, position and perspective. Obedience is simply to submit - and to submit simply means to accept another's will, or another person who is superior to you; to yield your will to them. Obedience then speaks of yielding, letting go of control. Obedience is to keep something that has been entrusted to you. It's to conform. It's to do as you are told. Fundamentally, this is what obedience is according to the Word of God.

To do as you are told, or to conform is not so much, the popular thing in our society. We are an individualistic society. Do you know why people are getting depressed - why depression has worked so well in our generation? Do you know why the rate of suicide has increased unbelievably in the last twenty years? Do you know why? We are an individualistic society, and on top of that, we have a society of - the philosophy of humanism. Most people's attitude today is, 'nothing else counts but me.' And then when nothing else is counting, because you closed your door to everybody, nobody can talk to you because you're too lofty. If you shut off all the channels of advice, then you will have nowhere else to go in times of trouble. God should be your refuge and strength, your shelter in the time of the storms.

I believe that one of the biggest losses of our times is what I refer to as convenient Christianity. This is where as believers we now only do things that suit our desires, ambitions and appetites instead of doing what Mary said to the men in the kitchen at the wedding in Cana in Galilee, *'whatever He tells you to do, just do it.'* This is a part of classical theology that we have lost in contemporary theology. The book of Revelations tells us that, *'they overcame him by the blood of the lamb, and the word of their testimony. Not only that, they loved not their lives even unto death.'* Sad to say that nowadays, people cannot even love their lives from the television in order to obey God.

Having defined what obedience is, I would like you now to consider some very simple and yet profound truths, which I believe, are the hallmarks of authentic obedience. These are foundational things that will help you determine whether or not you are operating in obedience according to the way the system was designed operate.

Obedience is not obedience until you obey.

Now that's pretty simple, isn't it? Obedience is not obedience until you obey or you act in line with the command in question. In the same way, change is not change until you change. You can talk about it. You can philosophise about. A bit like the Church has been doing - singing about it, dancing about it - but there is no power because we haven't changed yet. And all we have had is a form of godliness, but we denied the power thereof. There is no virtue in saying, 'Oh, I'm a changed man.' But you are still behaving the same way. *Albert Einstein said the definition of insanity is for a man to keep doing the same thing and expecting different results.* That is insanity. After thinking about this I thought, dear God, how many insane Christians have we got? How many insane husbands? I've been insane too. I have promised my wife that I am going to change in some area of my life. However, I still did the same thing and then expected different results. That is insane. Obedience is not obedience until you obey. Obedience is only obedience once you've acted in accordance with the demand that God places on your life.

Partial obedience is still disobedience.

Just doing half of the requirement is still disobedience. In ***1 Samuel 15: 22,*** the Lord had told and given Saul a command to go and kill Agag and all the people, and kill everything they had, but he was afraid of the people. The first thing that you have to deal with is the fear of man. You see, you cannot be a servant of God and be in bondage to people. The Apostle Paul wrote to the Galatians and said, *if I please men, I would not be a servant of Jesus Christ.* People will want you to do what suits them, but people's expectations change all the time. What they want today will not be the same thing they want tomorrow.

Therefore, if you are going to obey or be afraid of people you will not operate in God kind of obedience. Be released from the pressure of being in bondage to people. If you are going to obey God, it does not matter who says something, if what they say goes contrary to the Word of God. *It is better for us - Apostle Peter declared in* ***Acts 5****, for us to obey God than to please men.* At the end of the day it is God we are going to stand before on the Day of Judgement. Now I am not advocating rebellion or a lack of respect for authority, but that you have to make the Word of God the final authority in your life regardless of what anybody says.

Notice in Verse 17 of the same chapter what the prophet Samuel said to Saul, *'although you were once small in your own eyes, did you not become the head of the tribes of Israel? The Lord anointed you King over Israel, and He sent you on a mission saying go and completely destroy them'*. God commanded King Saul to completely destroy those Amalekites and make war on them until they were wiped out. In verse 19, the prophet said, *'but you did not obey the Lord your God because you pounced on the plunder and did evil in the sight of the Lord?* Notice King Saul's reply in verse 20. *'But I did obey the Lord'*. Just because he partially obeyed the commandment, he thought that he had obeyed God. The truth was he had brought back some of the plunder and also Agag the king.

Now, it was traditional in those days to spare the best of the spoils and the king, so you could offer sacrifices to the Lord and also parade the defeated king before one's subjects. Needless to say that if you are going to obey God, you may have to break with some of your traditions. Your traditions can make the Word of God of no effect. The other example is in ***Joshua 7,*** where Achan took some of the gold and silver contrary to the instructions from God. Jericho represented the first fruits of their inheritance. It was the first time they ever took possession of anything in the Land of Promise. Therefore everything including the best gold and silver didn't belong to them, it belonged to God. Why? Because if they gave everything to God that they took the first time they stepped into the Promised Land, the whole thing would become consecrated to the Lord, according to the established principle of *'First Fruits'*. The Bible teaches that, *'if the first fruits be holy, then the entire lump is holy', in Romans 11: 16.*

Notice what the prophet Samuel said to Saul in Verse 22. *'...Does the Lord delight in burnt offerings and sacrifices? God does not look at the outward appearance of the man. He always weighs the heart'*. The heart of a man weighs in the balance of the Lord's hands. God looks at the heart. Just because everybody was impressed did not mean that God was impressed too. To obey is better than sacrifice. In verse 23 the prophet said that *rebellion is like the sin of witchcraft and arrogance as evil as idolatry.* Rebellion is simply the same as pride. Basically, it is you saying, 'I'm going to do it my way'. Arrogance is then boasting about it and saying, 'I did it my way and I feel good, and nobody can stop me'. The prophet went on to also say *because you have rejected the Word of the Lord, the Lord has had no choice but to reject you also.* Oh, that's heavy.

Folks I'm telling you, there are Christians operating under a curse, because they have rejected the Word of God. God has no choice but to reject them. God did not go out there and put sickness on them. That is not what I am saying. What the scripture means is that God has withdrawn the covering, which His Word, the Name, the Blood and all of the essence of who He is, provide for all those who abide under the shadow of His wings. If you walk in disobedience to the Word of God you inevitably expose yourself to the wiles of the devil. If you play in the mud, you get dirty. If you play with the devil, he'll kill, steal and destroy all you got. It's not God's fault. That is just the way it is. How you treat the Word is how God will treat you.

Delayed obedience is still disobedience.

God is like the air traffic controller at the airport. He knows which planes are coming in from Amsterdam, which are coming in from London, which are coming in from New York, which ones are coming in from Sydney. He knows the exact position of each aeroplane and its place in the queue. He also assigns to each a landing time, which is equivalent to the point or timing of your obedience. But if you delay your landing time, you might have to go in circles for a while until He can re-arrange the schedule just for you. It is no wonder that Israel had to go round the same mountains for forty year until they had learnt obedience and the generation of unbelievers had all died.

Delayed obedience is still disobedience. Wonder why you still going through the same struggles? You should have gotten your breakthrough five years ago. If you aren't even obeying the written word of God, forget the specific will of God for your life. If you cannot obey what's already written down, why is He going to tell you the specifics of His Will for your life? If you are not faithful with little, you can't be trusted with much. You know, people say - 'Oh well, when I have more time I will come to church.' That's a lie. It is not what you are doing today that is causing you to fail to obey God; it is the attitude of your heart.

Jesus said, if you cannot obey in five pounds, for instance, you cannot obey with a thousand.

The Bible says that God is the teacher of profit. In other words, He will teach you how to increase in every area of your life. But if you keep failing the test, He cannot take you to great things. You see, God's not like our modern-day education system. You know, because you failed two, three, four times; they just pass you by, because you look stupid sitting in a little chair at fifteen years of age. No, That is not how heaven operates. You have to pass the obedience test before you move on. God is not a respecter of persons. You wonder why some Christians have been born again thirty years, and they're still children in understanding. The truth is that they have not passed the simple tests, and if you cannot do the elementary things - Paul said to the Corinthians - *'I couldn't even talk to you as spiritual.' All I could do was give you milk, because you were still children.'* I wonder what God has been trying to say to you, but because you have not passed simple tests of obedience, He has been restrained. Maybe He has wanted to tell you why that situation has not worked out yet, but because you are failing in little things, you blocked him out.

Oh, you mean God is that mean. He is not mean. You are the one that is mean because you are not willing to work the system. You are mean to yourself. You know people think, why did God say you robbed me in the tithe? Can a man rob God? Of course you cannot in the sense that you are not indispensable. But you know how you rob Him? You rob Him of the ability to do something good for you. It is like that child who decides to leave home when the father is the millionaire, and decides I'm going to go and make it on my own in order to get my own identity. Then he starts to live out of trashcans when the father owns a huge estate. He is robbing the father, not of his money, but of his ability to do something good for him. So God's not mean. We are mean to ourselves when we disobey God because we rob Him of the power to do something on our behalf that only He can do. It is time to reconsider and renew our minds where obedience is concerned. It is for our good and it is to our advantage that we obey God.

Chapter Four

Renewing Your Mind For Obedience

Romans 12: 2 says, *'do not be conformed to this world, but be transformed by the renewing of your mind, that you may prove what is that good and acceptable and perfect will of God.'* One of the most powerful things that could happen to any individual is the renewing of their mind. If you can change the way a person thinks, then you can change their outcomes in life. Obedience invariably starts with an attitude adjustment. Your perception of why obedience is necessary will shape your responses to the Word of God.

The degree to which you renew your mind by the word of God, the degree to which your thoughts, your ambitions, your desires, line up with the Word of God, is the same degree to which you will find it easy to obey God. If you line your mind up with the Word of God, it will not be nearly as hard to obey God, because your desires will be His desires. That is why you can delight yourself in the Lord, and He will grant you the desires of your heart. Your desires have become His desires. I believe that is what the bible means when it says, *'if you abide in me, and my word abides in you, ask whatsoever you will.'* The whatsoever you will after abiding, will have come in line with the Word of God, because you are clean through the Word. The Word of God cleans up all your desires.

The same degree of renewal will be the same degree of ease with which you will obey God. It won't sound like a big thing because you are in agreement with him already. Remember obedience is only necessary when in disagreement. Otherwise you are just acting lies. To the degree that you renew your mind is to the degree that you will find obedience easy. That means you are going to have to make the decision to make the Word of God your final authority. Let it be the place at which all arguments stop. However, if your mind is always going contrary to the Word of God, you will always have to fight yourself and later on the devil, in order to obey God. Let me tell you, God's way of teaching you is not necessarily through your circumstances.

God should always be able to get through to you, through your spirit. ***Proverbs 20: 22*** says, *'the spirit of the man is the candle of the Lord, searching the inward parts of the belly'*. In other words, God will use your spirit to direct your path - your Word is a lamp unto my path, and what a light unto my path. So He's saying I will direct you based on your spirit. If you are led by the spirit, you will always be in step with God. You can always lead a mistake free life. Do you know why we make mistakes? Because we do it our way. Being in step with the Holy Ghost every time keeps you walking into sweatless victories. He knows how to get every job done. Jesus said, 'I will show you who is like a wise man'. He didn't say, I will show you who is the wise man. He said I will liken Him unto a wise man. How? If He does what the wise man does. This means that if a person can get the leading of the wise man on the inside, he will get the wise man's results. Everybody will be thinking that that guy is pretty smart if he doesn't open his mouth. Why? Because he's doing what he sees the wise man do, and his house will always be established like that of the wise man.

If you are being taught by your circumstances, you need to know that that's the mercy of God. If the only time you listen is when it begins to go wrong, you will have so many things you could have avoided coming up in your life, because that's not the best way to be taught by God. God has not sent circumstances to teach you. Primarily, He sent His Word, and His Spirit. And people say, God does not do that but He will get the devil to put sickness on you, in order to teach you something. The devil is not the teacher of the Church, and he has nothing to do with how much you come to maturity. The devil doesn't want you mature, because when you mature, you are a candidate for your inheritance. The devil is not going to help you to get your inheritance. He is a thief - he is one that steals, kills and destroys. Therefore, don't give him credit for the things that God has brought you through. Renew your mind and then you won't wrestle with God.

God has declared the end from the beginning. The end is fixed. That's like showing up at a football match where you know that the final scores are fixed. God has already fixed the end. He has already declared it from the beginning. It sounds to me like even if you go around in circles, the destination will not change based on the route you take. The destination is still the same.

God is smarter than you and I are. And He has been around from everlasting to everlasting - He sure must have figured out some things more than you could ever do in your sixty, seventy, eighty or even ninety years. Foolishness is thinking that human wisdom is more accurate and relevant than the wisdom of God, which is His Word.

God already knows the end from the beginning. My end is fixed. Your end is fixed. Circumstances can do what they want to. I have permanent victory. Temporary delays in life do not bother me, because I know where I am going and it is an established destination. Therefore I set my heart on seeing the goodness of God, and His mercy following me all the days of my life. My end is fixed and I am not afraid of what tomorrow may bring, because I've got the Lord of tomorrow in my life. God has an established path for our lives. God has an established path to your destiny and obedience is your key to staying on it.

Every person who is honest enough with themselves can look back and say, if only I had obeyed God there, I probably would be ten thousand pounds in the black. If only I'd listened to my spirit, I would still have a good relationship with my children. If only I'd obeyed God, I would still have a sound mind. I wouldn't be having these sleepless nights. So much is riding on your obedience. The scripture calls the Word of God the perfect law of liberty. The purpose of the law of liberty is to bring freedom from everything that has hindered your advance until now. The key, however, is obedience. No wonder David declared, those that love the Lord and serve Him wholeheartedly only love themselves. Basically, God is going to do them good and bring them into sweatless anointing and victories.

Most Christians confuse submission with agreement. Obedience and agreement. *When in agreement, obedience is not necessary.* Obedience is only necessary when your will is contrary. Like any other natural or spiritual law, certain things have to be in place, before the law of exchange by obedience can begin to operate. For instance, with the law of gravity, if you are not standing on top of a building, you do not even have to worry about it at all because it is not necessary. Likewise, if you are in agreement, obedience is unnecessary. However, should you go out there and say, 'I don't believe the law of gravity is working, because I can't feel it', and jump off the top of a building, you will soon find out. The same is true with obedience. Just because you are in agreement doesn't mean you are obedient. Obedience isn't necessary for as long as you are in agreement.

Just because you do what you want to do, does not necessarily mean you submit to your husband. You see submission is when you want to go shopping at Meadowhall, but he wants to go the Trafford Centre. There is a difference. There is no way the two of you can be at both Meadowhall and Trafford Centre at the same time. And that is when submission or obedience comes into play. If you are in agreement, be careful that you don't mistake it for obedience. A lot of people think they obey their leaders and make their work a joy, like the book of Hebrews said. The reality though is that the leaders are doing everything they want them to do. They have said all the right things. They have done all the right things. They have supported all the right people and they've put on the right programmes. But the moment they don't agree with something, that's when you really find out whether or not they have learnt how to submit to authority.

By the way, the only things you should agree with are things that are done in line with the Word of God. So I don't care who is doing something, if they are not doing it by the Word, I'm not submitting to them because the Word of God should take precedence over any human authority. If your husband asks you to sin, don't do it in the name of submission. Most people get the shock of their life, particularly those who have just started dating. In the early days they do their best to impress and only show the partner their nice side, while carefully and masterfully hiding their ugly side. He may have a bad temper and also be quite selfish. He may detest being confronted and challenged too. He also maybe the kind that demands submission, even though he is not supposed to demand submission. The Bible teaches for us to submit one to another out of fear and reverence for Christ. There is not a single person who is beyond submission. I don't care even if he is the Very Reverend or the Archbishop, he should submit to somebody else out of fear and reverence for Christ.

We have to renew our minds because obedience is only necessary when your will is contrary to another. So, for you to say I obey God when you are doing what you would have loved to do anyway does not mean you are in obedience. You are simply in agreement. Often times we mistake obedience with agreement or submission with agreement, and then we think, maybe it's not God because it's too uncomfortable for us. The only thing this demonstrates is that you are not in agreement.

Obedience is when you want to go to Meadowhall to do your shopping, and then your husband says, I want us to go to the Trafford Centre. Being a limited commodity, who is not omnipresent, there is no way that you can be at Meadowhall as well as Trafford Centre. Based on where you end up going, we will be able to determine whether or not you are in obedience or disobedience. When you do what you wouldn't have done, that's when you obey God. Obedience is only necessary when there is conflict of wills.

Consider Jesus just before He went to the cross in the Garden of Gethsemane. During that time of agonising prayer, He said to God, *'Oh Father, if only you would let this cup, Pass me by.'* ***Matthew 26: 39.*** And then He said, *'But not my will, but your will be done.'* Maybe all this time he enjoyed raising the dead and letting the lame walk, and the blind see, and He didn't mind a little persecution, because He did what the anointing was on Him for. But then when He came to the crunch of why He came, He struggled with it. Obedience will always come with a struggle. If everything God told you to do, you do it with ease, either you have never stepped out of your comfort zone, or you are operating at half your capacity. Obedience will always cause you to count the cost. Jesus said, *'No man begins to build a tower without first counting the cost.'* No wonder David said, *'I wouldn't bring or give anything to the Lord that didn't cost me anything.'* Why?

Because if it doesn't cost you anything it's not worth anything at all. It is an honourable thing to yield your will to God especially when it is contrary to His will. However, the more excellent way is renewing your mind to where your will becomes His will. This will eliminate most of the struggles of an unrenewed mind.

One of the most liberating truths that I have found with regard to obedience is that, *God will never ask you to do for Him what He Himself is not prepared to do for you, and more.* God is not a killjoy. Do not let your mindset be like that of the man in Jesus' parable of the talents who buried his in the ground and when the Master enquired of it he said, *'Oh, Lord, I was so scared I hid your talent, because I know you are a ruthless man, who reaps, where he did not sow.* That's a lie. God's not reaping at all from where he did not sow. He is no man's debtor. God will never ask you to do more than He Himself is prepared to do for you because He is a covenant keeping God, who cannot deny Himself.

God will never ask you to do more than He is prepared to do for you. If God asks you for ten pounds, just know He is willing to give you ten thousand percent back. He said I will give you a hundredfold return. That's ten thousand percent. Have you ever thought about that? That's the purpose of the Word of God, to increase your life a hundredfold, to increase your marriage a hundredfold, to increase your health a hundred fold, to increase your finances a hundredfold. By the way, God is capable of more than a hundred fold return. The question is, can you believe for it? God will always reward you for your obedience.

Genesis 22 gives us the story of Abraham in which God said to him, 'Sacrifice your only son Isaac.' Isaac was a type of and shadow of Jesus Christ. He was born as the first-born son of promise. He was born out of Abraham's love for Sarah. He was the promised child, like Jesus was the begotten Son of the Father whom he loved. And He was the son of promise, the seed through which the nations or all the families of the earth would be blessed. And He asked Him at the very beginning to cut the covenant, to sacrifice his son, and the Bible says in the book of Hebrew, Abraham actually did sacrifice Isaac as in a figure and therefore received him back from the dead. As far as Abraham was concerned, Isaac was as good as dead.

The New Covenant or Testament as we know it was not started by Jesus. He confirmed and ratified it in His own blood, but the covenant roots are in the obedience of Abraham. It is also interesting to note that the same mountain range, Mount Moriah, is the same place where God sacrificed His Son Jesus on Calvary's cross. The same thing that God asked Abraham, his covenant partner, to do in the same mountain region, He also did to His own Son. And then He raised Him up from the dead, so that He could prolong His days, and that you and I could get in on the blessing of Abraham. That is why the scripture says that that He will do immeasurably more than you can ask or think.

God will never ask you to do more for Him than He is prepared to do for you. Why? Because He's a just God. He executes justice. He believes in balance. God has to reciprocate the action otherwise something would be missing in your life. It has to be both sides. So when God makes a demand for you to love your enemies and pray for those that despise you, He does not want you to just look stupid and let everybody walk all over you. He knows what He's doing. He's smarter than we are. Sad to say that often times, most of us do all the talking to somebody who knows everything. However, the most beneficial exercise you could ever embark on is that of renewing your mind.

Chapter Five

The Goodness & Faithfulness Of God

One of my favourite portions of scripture is **Exodus 19: 5 - 6,** which says, '*...if you willingly obey my voice and keep my covenant, then you shall be a special treasure to me above all people; for all the earth is mine. And you shall be to me a kingdom of priests and a holy nation. These are the words which you will speak to the children of Israel*'. Right at the beginning of the renewing of God's covenantal relationship with children of Israel, God made it clear to them that His intention was always to have them become the most treasured people on the face of the earth. However, the one condition for all these privileges was, obedience.

Two of the most liberating revelations that you can ever get as a child of God are; God is a good God and God is a faithful God who keeps His covenant even to a thousand generations. With such a realisation you will discover that God is completely trustworthy and dependable. Every time that I have struggled with obedience, the underlying question in my mind has always been, '*will God make His Word good to me?*' Can He be trusted to keep His side of the bargain? Is He dependable? Therefore, the issue where obedience is concerned is trust. Do you trust God enough to take Him at His Word? The Bible says, *'like a foot out of joint, so is a man that puts his trust in an unfaithful friend in the time of trouble'*. One of the hardest things to deal with is disappointment from a highly trusted friend. Have you ever been there? Thinking somebody will bail you out and then they fail you when you need them the most. But God is not like a foot out of joint. God is faithful.

God is trustworthy. He is worthy of all your trust. The primary reason, and this is the bottom line as to why people don't obey God, is that they don't trust Him. God is the only person who has guaranteed being true to His Word regardless and also He has the power to do so. He said, even *Heaven and Earth will pass away, but not one tittle or one iota will pass away from His Word.* Once He has given His Word, *it is forever settled in Heaven.* God's Word promises that, *even if you remain faithless, He will be faithful because He cannot deny Himself.* God is trustworthy. It is actually a dishonour to God when we disobey Him because we do not trust Him enough. We are really saying I am not convinced by your credibility. I am not sure I can believe the promises. That's the bottom line.

The measure of somebody's trustworthiness is what's in it for them. What they stand to gain from the transaction. Any time you trust someone, ask this question. What's in it for them? What do they stand to gain? Get a revelation of this; God is God all by Himself. So your presence in the picture does not either increase Him, or decrease Him. It does not make Him any more supreme. You can do whatever you want to, God will still be God. That is why He is trustworthy. Get that in your spirit. God is trustworthy. He is ever mindful of His covenant because He swore by Himself, seeing there was not one greater to swear by. He does not need your obedience in order to continue being God. God brings the counsel of the nations to nothing. His counsel stands forever, and yet in His goodness, He has chosen to share Himself and His creation with us.

Deuteronomy 10: 12. *'Now Israel, what does the Lord require of you but to fear the Lord your God, to walk in His ways and to love Him. To serve the Lord thy God with all your heart and with all your soul, to keep the Commandments of the Lord, and His statutes which I command you this day, for your good.*

Every time God asks me to do something, it's for my good. You see, when He says love your enemies, He is trying to save you from having all that unforgiveness to where you begin to develop even physical illnesses like arthritis, because bitterness has set in. The fear of the Lord is to keep His commandments. Walking in His ways is for us to walk according to His Word. Further, it says that the love of God is to keep His Commandments. Therefore, all the Lord requires of you and me is simple obedience According *to **1 John 5: 3b,** God's Commandments are not burdensome.*

God said that if you keep my Commandments, it's for your good. The word good comes from the same root word as 'please', which comes from the same root word that means prosperity, which means wholeness, which means soundness, which means completion. To have 'nothing missing and nothing broken', God said we must keep His Word. God did not give us His Word so we can miss out on the good things in life. He is not a killjoy. He has given us His Word so that there can be nothing missing and nothing broken in our lives.

Psalms 37: 3 - 4. *'Trust in the Lord and do good; Dwell in the land and feed on His faithfulness. Delight yourself also in the Lord, and He shall give you the desires of your heart.'*

Obedience is for my own good. Trust in the Lord. That's the bottom line. Trusting the Lord. Do good, so that you may dwell in the land and you shall be fed. Delight yourself in the Lord. Delight yourself in the Lord. The root word for *delight* there simply means this; be like clay in the potter's hand; be pliable in the potter's hand. Don't be like the clay Jeremiah prophesied about that even had the audacity to say to its maker, why do you fashion me like this? Be pliable. Just yield to Him and say shape me Lord. I'm on the wheel. Just do what you want to do. Shape me Lord. This is my will. It's for my good. God's promise to you is that, if you become pliable, He'll grant you the desires of your heart.

Delighting yourself in the Lord will cause the goodness and mercy of God to follow you all the days of your life. Delighting yourself in the Lord will deliver you from chasing things and instead, things will start chasing you. Therefore, quit chasing the things. Just go after God. *If you seek first the Kingdom and all His righteousness, then all these things shall be added unto you.* God can be trusted because even what you would have gone for He is going to give you if you go after Him. So what have you got to lose in obeying God? Preferring temporary comfort and instant gratification are marks of immaturity.

You may well say, 'oh, I've been tithing ten years and I haven't really seen the devourer rebuked on my behalf. I guess I will just stop tithing'. All right. What else did He say about that scripture? He said, remember all the way I led you through all the wildernesses, and I delivered you from snakes, scorpions and things that could have taken your life, even when you were young. Other people went through all kinds of things but you were protected from most calamities. All this is part of your honouring of God. Just because your bills are not paid yet, does not mean that you should stop tithing. Do not be short-sighted. Obeying God is for your own good.

God can completely be trusted. David said, *'as for God, His ways are just and His work is perfect*. Then Moses also said, *'ascribe greatness to our God the rock, His Work is perfect and all His ways are just. He is a God of faithfulness and all His works are done in justice.'* Therefore, God is completely trustworthy. Why? Because God is good. Make up in your mind, God is good to me and His goodness is not dependent upon what I go through in life. It is solely dependent on the fact that He said He is and He is not a man that He should lie. Take him at his word. There is power in embracing such a revelation.

God's goodness and faithfulness transcend time. His goodness has gone beyond the veil. He's not limited by time and space. From everlasting to everlasting, He has always been God and

He has always been good. Why? Because God's too perfect to change. If He had to change, He would have to either digress or regress - increase or decrease. If He decreased, it would mean that He was too much. If He increased, it would mean that He was less than He should have been. That's why you can expect Him to be there for you, all the time. He's always the same. God's plan is already blessed. God is good. He is not the dammar; He's the Redeemer. He's not the one that's making you sick. God is the healer. He sent Jesus to heal your broken heart. Jesus came that you might have life and have it more abundantly. Do not let men's theology and philosophies deceive you and misrepresented God. God is good from ever lasting to ever lasting.

The bottom line, why people struggle with obedience, is they don't believe to see the goodness of the Lord. David said in ***Psalm 27: 13***, *'I would have fainted unless I had believed to see the goodness of the Lord in the land of the living.'* You ought not to be of them that faint, that shrink back and are destroyed. You're supposed to be a person of hope, because you are not a stranger to your covenant. You ought to know that your God is good, and that He keeps His covenant even to a thousand generations.

Somebody said what's goodness? Goodness is being able to be alive, when the doctor said you should have been dead. Goodness is being able to expect to be out of debt. Goodness is being able to expect to walk with a sound mind, with all your needs met, with your family restored. That's the goodness of the Lord. Surely goodness and mercy shall follow me all the days of my life. In ***Jeremiah 29: 11,*** God said *'I know the plans* *that I have for you. Plans to prosper and not to harm you; plans to prosper you and give you a future.'* God knows the thoughts, the plans that He has towards you. In ***Ephesians 2: 10***, from the amplified Bible it says, *'For we are God's own handiwork, His workmanship created in the anointed Jesus, born anew, that we may do those good works, which God planned, predestined, beforehand, for us, taking parts which He prepared ahead of time, that we should walk in them, living the good life.'*

God has already prepared for each of His children, the *'good life.'* You see people have been turning their backs on God, pursuing the good life. But He says here, 'Before time began God had purposed; planned that you should have the good life.' You were not destined to be poor, broken down, disgusted and busted; you were destined to live the good life. God is good. Understanding the goodness and faithfulness of God will set you free from spending all your life chasing after things.

Do you remember when the rich young ruler came to Jesus in ***Mark 10?*** He asked Him, *'what must I do to inherit the Kingdom of heaven?'* Jesus told him to observe the Law of Moses, to which he replied, *'all these have I done since my youth'*. Jesus said to him, *'you've done all these things, but one thing you lack.'* He said, 'There's only one thing between you and eternal life.' Now eternal life in this verse does not mean, living forever. The root Greek word there is *Zoë, the God's kind of abundant life*. The one thing between you and the God kind of abundant life is that you are making money your master instead of making

God your master. That is why Jesus said, *'It is difficult for those that are rich, to get into the Kingdom of God.'* And everybody preached saying don't be rich, because you'll miss out on the Kingdom of God. *'It is easier for a camel to go through the eye of a needle.'* Not knowing the history of that scripture, that the eye of the needle was the small opening in the gates to the city, and not the literal meaning of the word needle, most Christians missed the whole crux of the matter. Jesus didn't mean that you couldn't get into the Kingdom of God.

Anyway, Peter then turned around and said, *'Lord, we've left everything.'* And just in case you didn't know, Jesus said, 'I tell you the truth.' *'Anybody who's left houses, mothers, fathers, brothers and sisters, lands, anything, for my sake and for the Kingdom - will, not in Heaven - will in this life, receive a hundredfold with persecution.'* I believe the persecution part will be from those Christians who want to pretend that they do not just as much spend time praying about money as everybody else who is broke. Get God in the equation. God is good. Obedience is not a way for God to short-change you. It is the doorway to the good life.

There are other factors that we should consider when dealing with the question of obedience. God once said to me, *'if you want me to be faithful to you, you ought to become faithful because to the faithful, I have to show myself faithful.'* Where a spouse is concerned, it is of uttermost importance for you to both agree that you would make the Word of God your final authority. To the degree that you both become dependable to God is the degree to which you will be worthy of each other's trust. You cannot put your spouse before God. This applies to friendships too. To the degree that you are faithful to God is to the same degree, to which you will be faithful to your fellow human beings. The degree to which you obey God is the degree to which you are worthy of trust.

The bottom line to the covenant is trust. The only reason Abraham could raise up the sword over his only son, who was the hope of his inheritance; was because he trusted God. It is recorded in the book of Hebrews that Abraham believed God that He would even raise him up from the dead, if that's what it was going to take. He without a doubt knew that God is trustworthy. Abraham reasoned, even if I sacrifice Isaac, something else is going to come up for my good.

God is not prepared to ask more from you in terms of obedience and sacrifice, than what He is prepared to do for you. God is no man's debtor. Notice, that when Abraham demonstrated unequivocal obedience to God, He obligated God to do the same thing on the cross of Calvary with His only Son Jesus. However, God had to take it a step further. Unlike Isaac, Jesus literary died. When you understand this principle, you will enter into God's rest because you will know that every time God asks for obedience, it is because He wants to do something better for you. God wants to give whatever you sacrifice back to you in good measure, pressed down, shaken together and running over. Do not let fear rob you of the opportunity to come up higher as you walk through the door of obedience. God is a good God and His faithfulness endures to all generations. There is neither variableness nor shadow of turning in Him. God has always been and will always be good and faithful because He cannot deny Himself.

Chapter Six

Understanding Your Inherent Advantage

The two biggest lies of the devil in the area of obedience are; firstly, that God may not keep His promise to you. Secondly, that you may be short-changed if you keep obeying what God tells you to do. In this chapter I am going to focus on the latter deception. I will endeavour to show you the inherent advantage that is released through your obedience to God. We are going to examine God's intentions for admonishing you and I to keep His commandments. We are going to get revelation of the fact that the word of God was not written for our disadvantage. Instead, it was written in order that it might be well with you and your children, that you might live the God kind of abundant life, and that you might prolong your days.

God's word was not written for your disadvantage. I'll say it again. Settle it forever that God's word was not written or given for your disadvantage. There is not one single scripture that is there with the intention of putting you at a disadvantage. However, it is going to take a lot of courage to obey the Word of God.

In ***Deuteronomy 5: 29 - 33***, listen to God's heart. The background is that the children of Israel had come up to the mountain, and God had told them to wash their clothes for three days. After these three days, they were to come and hear His word. They could not however stand in His presence because they were terrified of Him. They thought that the awesomeness of His presence would kill them. So they settled for Moses being their representative. They said to Moses, 'you go and talk to God.' Moses then walks into the presence of God and tells God that the people were afraid of coming into His presence because of their disobedience.

Moses was displeased as he reported this to God saying, 'Look, God, they don't want to come and meet with you. What's wrong with them?' In reply, God said to Moses, *'Oh, that there was such a heart in them that they would fear me and keep my commandments; That it may be well with them; that it might be well with their children.'* You could just feel God's heart bleeding. That's what happens every time you disobey God. He says, 'Oh that you had such a heart, that you would fear me and then it would be well with you and your household. God's plans for your life are good and therefore, His Word was not written or given for your disadvantage.

If you establish you heart in this truth, you will never be afraid to obey God. Settle this truth forever. Everything you see in the Word of God, even if you do not understand the reason why you should do it just do it. Take comfort in the truth that God is smarter than you are and His plans for your life are good. Settle this forever, the word of God was not written for your disadvantage. The word of God does not come so that you can be disadvantaged. Obedience unleashes your inherent advantage. It opens you up to partake of the goodness and compassion of God. Now, let us consider this portion of scripture.

Deuteronomy 5: 29 & 33. *'Oh that there was such a heart in them, that they would fear me, and keep all my commandments always, that it might be well with them and their children forever. Ye shall walk in all the ways which the Lord your God commanded you, that ye may live and prolong your days in the land which ye shall possess.'*

There is such tremendous power to be tapped into by those who are willing to obey God. The word of God was not written for your disadvantage. Notice God's heart, stemming out of His goodness and compassion, saying, *'Oh that there was such a heart in them.'* You can even feel God's yearning saying, I just wish you could trust me. In the above scripture, I believe that God has revealed more of His heart for His people concerning the purpose of the Word in their lives. Let us consider them individually.

1. God's word was written so that it might be well with you. The words 'being well' or 'well-being' come from the same root word in Hebrew that means peace, prosperity, wholeness, and soundness. So when He says, 'Oh that you would obey that it might be well with you.' He means, I want you to obey my Word so that you may prosper; so that you may be sound;

so that you may be complete; so that you might have nothing missing and nothing broken. Oh, that you would obey my Word.

2. ***That it might be well with their children.***

Based on your obedience, the same things that are available to you will be available to your children. That's why, when people say, I have no place for the Word of God, I have graduated from the Word of God, I say you've graduated from your soundness. You've graduated from your prosperity. In the book of ***Lamentations 3: 17,*** the prophet Jeremiah wrote, *'You have removed my soul far off from peace; I forgot prosperity.'*

Now realise that what produces well-being or prosperity is the Word of God. Most people have been looking for health at the doctors, looking for soundness from their psychologist, looking for provision from their bank manager, looking for security from their insurance company, looking for significance from their job, looking for peace from whatever they have chosen to put their trust in, but here the Word of God is declared as the source of your well being. Jeremiah is lamenting, crying, and weeping saying, *'and thou art removed my soul far from peace, from wholeness, because I forgot prosperity, I forgot well being.'* God's Word is the true source of well-being. How did they forget well-being? Through their disobedience.

We need to cultivate a right attitude towards the Word of God. ***Hebrew 2: 1 - 3*** says, *'therefore we must give the more earnest heed to the things we have heard, lest we drift away.... How shall we escape* *if we neglect so great salvation, which first began to be spoken by the Lord, and was confirmed to us by those who heard Him.'* Notice what he is saying. It is the same thing that the prophet Jeremiah was saying to the folks in the Old Testament. The writer to the Book of Hebrews says the same thing to the New Testament Christians. He says, *'therefore we ought to give the more earnest heed to these things.'* In other words we ought to pay attention to these things - to the Word that we have received, that we have heard, lest we should let it slip.

You can let the Word of God slip through your fingers with your eyes wide open, the consequence of which is a lack of wholeness. We lack prosperity when we forget the Word of God. It is the Word of God, which causes us to be sound and complete. Therefore, God says be careful. You cannot be careless about how much of the Word of God you hear because if you forget the Word you will forget peace. And if there's no peace, then something is missing and something is broken. You can be different from those people who are not party to the covenants of promise. They are without hope or God in this world. Obedience is the key to the well-being of both you and your household.

The writer went on further to say in verse 2, *'for if the word which was still spoken by angels, was steadfast, and every transgression and disobedience received a just recompense of reward, how shall we escape?'* He is basically saying, 'what makes you think you are so special? Oh, I'm a New Testament Christian. I'm born again; I have got my ticket to Heaven. But, what's the use of just having hope for the future when you are going through Hell on Earth? What kind of witness is that? How shall we escape, he says, if we neglect so great salvation? The same root meaning of the word peace, which Jeremiah used, is now translated salvation, in this passage. It still means wholeness, and healing and deliverance, which come from the Word of God.

How shall we escape? How shall it be different for you and your household if you forget the Word of God? If you choose not to obey the Word, how shall you escape the diseases? However shall you escape the distress, and the trials of life? Everything around us is falling apart. There's more abuse and drugs and every kind of junk in our days, than there was in the days of our forefathers. How shall we escape? You need to be serious about reversing the trend and the only way you can escape is through obeying God. When you talk about escape, you're not talking about an easy ride. The writer to the book of Hebrews is talking to Christians. How will you escape, Christian, if you neglect the Word of God? If you let 'So great salvation' slip. It will be well with you if you keep the Word of God. You can and will escape.

It is important at this stage to also point out that you cannot keep what you do not know. How shall we escape? It's going to be well with you based on the Word of God. It is not going to be well with you based on your high expectations, because that's just hope that is not founded on the Word of God and it might be just some encouraging facts that you are putting your trust in. Only the Word of God is the truth and the truth will change the facts, but the facts will not change the truth. Keep the Word of God for it is life to those that find it and health to all their flesh.

3. ***You shall walk in all the ways which the Lord your God has commanded you, that you may live'.***

The third reason why God gave us His Word is so that we might live. When the Bible talks about living, it does not mean inhaling and exhaling. It is talking about the God kind of abundant life. *'Forsake your ways and come up higher and your ways are not my ways and your thoughts are not my thoughts, but come up higher, according to* ***Isaiah 55****.'* God started off this chapter of Isaiah by saying that somethings you cannot buy with money. You do not have to be loaded to have this kind of 'stuff'. You do not have to be educated to have this kind of 'stuff'. My Word is a level playing field. The Word of God was given to deliver you from living beneath your covenant privileges.

When you are tired of simply being a mere man and just hanging out here in the natural realm, the Word of God will be the instrument that will propel you to higher ground. When you are tired of being limited to the dictates of your education, social class, income bracket and back-ground; when you are tired of being the tail and want to be the head, then the key will be your obedience to the word of God. When you are tired of your healing being dictated by the present medical instruments and what treatments the doctors have found, then obeying the Word of God will cause it to become health to all your flesh. You do not have to raise your children based on what you learned from your forefathers, because, bless their hearts, however much they did, they never had to go through some of the junk that is happening at the moment. You need the wisdom of God to let you know, how to train up a child in the way that it should go. Then I believe it will be well with your children.

Do not become too comfortable with low existence, as if you have not got a blood-sworn covenant. God said in blessing, I will bless you. No matter how blessed you feel, even in blessing, in the midst of you feeling like you've got something, you can still increase. And if you don't want to increase because you are comfortable, you are a selfish person. You don't know what's at stake. Somebody might never go to Heaven because you stayed broke. It just doesn't take speaking in tongues to preach the Word of God. You should therefore desire to go up higher. Make it your goal to look back over your life and see that you have done some things that they said you couldn't do, because you didn't have that level of intelligence. You obeyed the Word of God and nobody could keep you down. It is time for you to move from the land of just enough, to go to the land of more than enough. Your days of sleepless nights can be over by the Word because it declares that, '*He grants His beloved sleep. He that watches over you neither sleeps nor slumbers*', so you can rest. You are not a limited man. You have got access to the supernatural power of God and it is released by your obedience to the Word of God.

John 3: 21a Jesus said, '*he that doeth the truth will come to the light.*' He that does the Word of God will always come to the light. In other words, *the entrance of God's Word brings light.* The Word makes you see what was there already, but because it was dark, you couldn't see it. He that doeth the truth will come to the light. In other words, it is just as if you took a coke and put it under water, as soon as you release it, it rises straight to the top. They put you through hell, they sack you on the job, it doesn't matter, and you still rise to the top. They say no, you are too this, you are too that, you cannot do that, you cannot come here. Yet as you continue doing the truth, you come to the light. Always above and not beneath. Forever the head and not the tail. Why? Because the Word of God is taking you to a higher plain.

When God said, *'oh that they would fear me and keep my commandments'*, He was saying oh that they could pack their bags and get out of the land of sorrow, and get out of the land of just being limited to their I.Q. So they could do exploits and mighty things. So they can do things that they had never seen anybody do before. The land where they could begin to do the greater works that Jesus said they were capable of.

4. ***If you obey me, you will prolong your days.***

The fourth reason why God gave us His Word was so that we may prolong our days. The Word of God was not written for your disadvantage. God wants you to prolong your days. You do not have to die young. *With long life God will satisfy you and show you His great salvation*. If you keep doing the Word, you will prolong your days. How do I know if I have had a long life? Until I am satisfied. They can have all kinds of accidents etc, none of your bones will be broken. Confess ***Psalm 91*** everyday so that the reality of that scripture becomes alive in your spirit man. You have angels with charge over you lest you dash your foot against the stones and none of your bones will be broken. A thousand may fall at your side and ten thousand at your right hand, but it will not come near you. In spite of all these diseases in the world, God is your refuge and strength.

He said that *if you serve Him, He would bless your bread, He would bless your water, none of you will miscarry nor be barren, sickness will be taken from the midst of you and the number of your days, He would fulfil,* ***Exodus 23: 25 - 26***. You don't have to die young. Trust the Lord and choose not to lean on your own understanding. But in all your ways acknowledge Him and He will make your paths straight. Learn to obey the Word. It was not written for your disadvantage, instead it was written in order that it might be well with you and your children, that you might live the God kind of abundant life, and that you might prolong your days. Unlock your inherent advantage through obedience.

Chapter Seven

The Door To The Secret Counsel Of God

The Apostle Paul wrote to the Churches at Corinth and said that since there was still strife and division among them, they were acting as mere men. In other words, they should have been able to function as supernatural men. The issue was not the strife in which He found them, but the disobedience that was behind the strife. Consequently, they could not access the power, the anointing and the wisdom of God, which would have allowed them to function as supernatural men. The wisdom of God is an indispensable ingredient for one's prosperity and good success.

Obedience is the doorway to the secret counsel of God. God has got a million and one ways to meet your needs according to His riches by Christ Jesus. However, we have been so indoctrinated by the world into thinking that our success is based upon our education, the kind of jobs that we have, and whatever kind of things they have put in that equation. The

Bible says that, *'wisdom is the principal thing; therefore get wisdom and in all your getting, get understanding.* ***Proverbs 4:7.*** Notice the scripture did not say that wisdom is part of the principal thing. It said that, ***wisdom is the principal thing***. Therefore your success is not going to be based on what academic degrees you have or haven't got. It's going to be by the anointing of wisdom and if Christ the anointed one, and His anointing, be in you, He is your hope, your earnest expectation of Glory.

Most people live limited lives that are full of dead-ends. They can only go so far before they hit the brick wall. They are constrained in so many ways. They wonder why things that were impossible before they made Jesus the Lord of their lives are still impossible. The truth is that there is not a single thing that you cannot have in this life, if you get the secret counsel of God. God is the source of all that you will ever need for life and godliness. However, the exchange will be your obedience. It is going to cost you. More often than not, most people want to be anointed on the cheap. You cannot exchange the deeper for the cheaper. The anointing is not cheap. Wisdom is not cheap. Obedience is the exchange that lets you into the secret counsel of God.

Obedience is the doorway to the secret counsel of God. Most of you are pleading with God for specific directions in your life and ministry. God will be more willing to talk to you about the specific details of your assignment after you obey the general details. The Bible says that the counsel of God, the secret counsel of God is with those who fear Him. How do we know they fear Him? By keeping His word. Jesus said, I call you my friend if you keep my commandments. ***Psalm 25: 14*** says that *'the Lord confides in those who fear Him.'* What is the fear of the Lord? The fear of the Lord is to depart from evil; it's to keep His commandments; it's to obey Him. The Lord said that if you obey Him, He would begin to confide in you. The Bible talks about God being the teacher of profit. He is the teacher of increase. He would teach you how to get the wealth of the secret place. He is going to confide in you, and say, do you know, if you drive down to such and such a place you will come across that million pound deal you have been looking for. He will give you concepts, insights and ideas that will cause you to maximise your potential in all that He created you to be.

The Bible says that God would give you wisdom for witty inventions. The wisdom of God is available to any man because God gives it liberally to all who dare to ask for it. But obedience is the key to the secret counsel. The Lord confides in those who fear Him. Remember God did not say that He would give you money but instead He would give you the power to get wealth. The power that will get wealth is the counsel, the secret counsel of God. It will flow through ideas, insight and concepts. The scripture says in the night-time your heart, your spirit man, will instruct you. Some people today are getting by with just enough, when they could have a whole lot more if they obeyed God. *God wants to lead you to your wealthy place, according to* ***Psalm 66: 12.*** It's time to get rid of this mindset of having more faith in our natural abilities than we have in the wisdom of God.

We need to renew our minds. It is possible to have access to the secret counsel of God if you obey Him. You do not have to go through your life based on your abilities when you can tap into the secret counsel. With such wisdom you can rest assured that it is going to be well with you and your children because you are not operating as just a natural man, but as one who has inside information regardless of what you are dealing with.

John 7: 17. *'If anyone chooses to do the will of God,[chooses to obey me], he will find out whether or not my teaching comes from God, or whether I speak of my own self'.* In other words, without obedience you won't have any insight into the Word of God. Most Christians are bored when they attempt to study the Word of God because they do not get any revelation knowledge out of it. By failing to obey the general principles of the Word, they also forfeit the privilege of receiving God's secret counsel. Revelation knowledge into the Word of God is connected to your obedience. Jesus said for you to know that what He taught was from God, you must obey Him first. It also says in Scripture that He told the men who wanted to see signs and wonders, *'take my Word first and then you will see miracles, signs and wonders.'* That's why it says in ***Matthew 13: 12*** that, *'whoever has, to him more will be given, and he shall have abundance; but whoever does not have, even what he has will be taken away from him.'* To him that obeys, more revelation from the Word will come.

Hebrews 5: 12 - 14. The writer to the Hebrews says, *'Even though you ought to be teachers by now, you need someone to teach you the elementary truths of God's Word all over again. You need milk, not* *solid food. Anyone who lives on milk being still an infant is not acquainted with the teaching about righteousness. But solid food is for the mature, who by constant use [continued obedience], have exercised their senses to discern between good and evil'.* You can discern which way God is leading you, if you obey God. It's like working out. Some of you are not spiritual giants yet, because you are not working out on the elementary truths. When you exercise, you're working out.

Sometimes you will have to work out, practice doing what is right - obedience - even if you don't feel like it because you are cultivating consistency. Consistency will eventually bring maturity. Maturity will breed fortitude. The Bible says that *if a strong man guards his house, then his possessions are safe.* Let there never be a time when the devil comes and he is stronger than you are. Always work out in the spirit. I'm working on something so that there will never be a time when the devil comes in and he is stronger than I am. Remember the scripture in ***Isaiah 59*** that most people have translated wrongly. It says that, *'when the enemy shall come in,* most people say like a flood - that's not what it says. *'When the enemy shall come in - the Bible says, like a flood, the Lord will raise the standard against him.* The wisdom of God will cause you to be stronger than your adversaries. The Bible says that by wisdom, Kings wage war.

Apart from discovering the secret counsel of God, obedience will put you in place where the anointing of God will flow in and out of your life effortlessly. I like to refer to this perpetual flow as a *sweatless anointing.* There is overwhelming evidence of this kind of *sweatless anointing* operating in the lives of all those who were willing to take God at His Word. Examples of this include, Isaac sowing seed in a time of famine and reaping a hundred fold in the same year; Jacob being willing to do with the cattle according to the wisdom revealed to him by God, hence becoming so wealthy and powerful to the point that Laban's sons and servants became jealous; Elijah outrunning Ahab's finest horses and chariots on bare feet; The widow at Zarephem who baked a cake for the Man of God and ended up being sustained with her son by the anointing of multiplication for three and half years; One of the sons of the prophets, whose axe head fell into the water and Elisha by the anointing, causing the axe head to float; Daniel's life being spared in the lion's den; The three Hebrew boys' lives not being consumed by the fiery furnace; Peter casting the nets into the deep at Jesus' Word, in spite of his fruitless efforts all night, and ending with a net-breaking, boat-sinking catch; The servants at the wedding that Jesus attended in Cana having their water turned into wine because they heeded Mary's instruction of, whatever He tells you to do, just do it; The people at Lazarus' tomb obeying the instruction of rolling the stone away; The ten lepers that were cleansed as they were on the way to show themselves to the High Priest. The list goes on and on.

Suffice to say that, to the degree that we become willing to obey God is to the degree that He will release His anointing without measure on our lives. The anointing is an indispensable ingredient of a victorious life. By definition, the anointing is that burden removing, yoke destroying power of God. Once God has given you the wisdom to know what the root of the matter is in any given situation, you then need the anointing of God to make every situation line-up with God's will for you. Every time God gives a Word, there is enough anointing in that Word to cause itself to come to pass in your life. Obedience to God's Word releases the anointing that is contained in that Word.

Jesus categorically stated that whatever He said and did was what His Father had told Him to say and what He saw the His Father doing. In other words, Jesus walked in perfect submission and obedience to God. In ***John 3: 34,*** the Bible says that, *'He spoke the Word of God, therefore, God anointed Him with Spirit without measure.'* Notice how speaking the Word, or more specifically completely obeying the Word of God, put Jesus in a position where the anointing could flow without hindrance in His life. He always had sweatless victories because He was willing to act on the instructions that He received from His Father. If ever there was a time when the body of Christ needed to walk in that anointing without measure, it is now. There are more burdens on people's lives than ever before. Mere religion will not do it for people. We need the power from on High to come upon us and remove every burden and destroy every yoke in people's lives. The key, however, is obeying God. Without obedience, none of us qualify for the anointing.

There are times, though, that people stay anointed even if they have disobeyed God. The reason is that the anointing on any of our lives is not for us but for the people to whom we are ministering. Consequently, being anointed is not a validation of one's character and integrity. I believe that it is impossible to sustain an anointed life without obedience. Most preachers then turn to using gimmicks and other props to keep the ministry flowing. However, there is no substitute for the anointing because after a while the people will start noticing that nothing has changed in their lives with any degree of significance. Just like it will take obedience to be privy to the secret counsel of God, it is also going to take obedience to walk in that anointing without measure. However, both wisdom and anointing are available to anybody who is willing to make the exchange through their obedience.

Chapter Eight

The Key To Intimacy With God

My fundamental conviction is that the missing ingredient in most people's lives is intimacy with God. Intimacy is an indispensable quality for a fulfilled life. In an effort to substitute this vital life ingredient, countless millions, Christians and non-Christians alike, have turned to a continuum of alternatives.

Personally, I believe that broken fellowship with God, or separation as the Bible calls, is the fundamental issue that is causing mankind to self-destruct. Ironically, even most born again, spirit filled Christians have never known the tenderness of God's embrace and the softness of His presence. Emptiness, depression and loneliness have been the hallmarks of their experience. Sometimes there is no better way to describe the experience of most people than by the words of the Apostle Paul in Ephesians chapter two. He said that some people are strangers to the covenants of promise, without hope or God in this world. This sad scenario is both true for Christians and non-Christians alike. Sadly, most people are still looking for this missing ingredient of intimacy in the wrong place. Simplicity, however, is the greatest key to soundness in God.

Obedience is the thing that creates intimacy with God. Most people would not even know what was wrong with them if it were not for the Word of God. When the Bible says, Adam knew his wife; the Hebrew word there means to be *intimately involved and acquainted with*. The kind of knowledge, that when you come together you produce something. So when we know God, God wants us to know him in such a way that every time we come together with Him we can produce something. We can produce healing, if that's what we need. We produce wealth, we produce wholeness, and we produce restoration, if that's what we need.

Consider any natural relationship. How would you like to have a friend who every time you asked them to do something for you, they didn't oblige? There would be no pleasure in that relationship. **John 15: 14**, Jesus told His disciples, *'you are my friends if you do what I command you'*. Notice, He didn't say you are my disciples; He said you are my friends. The word friendship, in this context, is born out of covenant. The Bible says Abraham was the friend of God. Now friendship means intimacy. You can be His son; you can be His servant; you can be anything you want to be, but in order to qualify for His friendship, you have to be doing what He tells you to. The Bible says that He is a friend that sticks closer than a brother.

Obedience ushers you into the realm of intimacy with God. *This intimacy even causes God to be comfortable enough to confide in you, according to* ***Psalm 25: 14.***

Abraham was God's friend, and now he is the father of us all. Why? Because he did what God told him to do. The scriptures tell us that *Abraham believed God and it was credited to him as righteousness,* according to ***Genesis 15: 6.*** Friendship with God will boost your confidence. Confidence that God will be there when you need Him to meet every need; confidence that God will answer my prayers; confidence that when you lay your hands on the sick they will recover; confidence that when you cast out devils the person will be set free; confidence that when you declared that you are out of debt, God's angels will go to work. The only thing that guarantees such boldness is obedience. With such confidence, you can also rest in the comfort of knowing that *even though your mother and father forsake you, according to* ***Psalm 27: 10,*** *yet the Lord will receive you.* You are His friend.

John 15: 10. I*f you obey my commandments you will abide in my love just as I have kept my father's commandments and abide in His love.* There are two things that Christians confuse. They confuse relationship and fellowship. You can be in relationship with God, but you can have broken fellowship. When you are in relationship with God, you are born again, but if you have lost your fellowship with God, you lose the intimacy that comes with knowing that God is there and that is what Jesus is talking about in the above scripture.

Obedience will cause you to remain in the Love of God. Now we know, it's a fact and it's the truth, that God loves everybody in the world exactly the same way. However, not everybody has access, or has the same ability to tap into His perfect love, outside of the realm of simple obedience. Obedience bridges the gap so to speak. It takes you from the general, from the crowd, into the individual treatment.

A person who is intimate with God, can love unconditionally. People who are intimate with God naturally have passion for His eternal purposes in the earth. A church that is intimate with God can speak well of each other, and there is always a sense of I belong, because there is no fear in love.

John 14: 21 says, *'whoever has my commandments and obeys them, it is he who loves me, and he who loves me will be loved by my Father. And we will come to him and make our abode with him'*. There is preferential treatment for those who walk in obedience. Now do not misunderstand me, God loves everybody. However, what He's saying is that you will be given preferential treatment because to the faithful, God has an obligation to show Himself faithful.

Jesus said that He and the Father would come and make their abode with you. Based on your obedience God is going to hang out at your house. Obedience keeps you in the manifest presence of God. Therefore with obedience, all things that cannot exist in His presence will leave you and your household alone. Restoration, hope, provision and healing will show up because the manifest presence of God is in your midst. Everything in your house will change to reflect His glory. Remember, *where the Word of the King is, according to Ecclesiastics, there is power.*

One of the most frequent questions that I get is, 'how can I measure whether or not I am intimate with God?' Sometimes we can talk about being holy, but if we don't define the subject matter and set out some criteria, we can feel either condemned, or so good, or we might not even know what to feel like. Let us consider what the Psalmist said in ***Psalm 84.*** Listen to a man that was intimate with God. *How lovely are your dwelling place, oh Lord, Almighty. My soul yearns.* When did you last yearn to be in God's presence? *My soul yearns, even faints for the courts of the Lord, and my flesh cry out for the living God. Even the sparrow has found a home and the swallow a nest for herself, where she may have her young. A place near your altar, oh Lord, Almighty, my King, my God. Blessed are those who dwell in your house. They are ever praising you.* He's actually saying, the man who is always praising God is blessed.

Most Christians cannot even stand singing the same song more than once. They say, 'oh I don't want to sing - if I sing that song another time, I'm going to explode'. How would you like to be one of the twenty four elders, who since their creation only worship God saying, Holy, holy, holy, is the Lord, who was, and is, and is to come.

Yearning to be in the presence of God. He says, *blessed are those whose strength is in you, who have set their hearts on pilgrimage as they pass through the valley of Baca, they make the place a spring of water, the autumn also covers it with pools. They go from strength to strength.* Notice what intimacy with God creates. You go from strength to strength, until each appears before Zion, till you stand before God.

Notice David's passion in verse 10. *Better is one day in your courts than a thousand elsewhere. I'd rather be a doorkeeper.* David said even if I am only a steward, just to stand at the door in the house of God, is better than being in the house of the wicked. I just want to be where He is. Just close to Him. I'd rather be a doorkeeper. That just stirred me up. The man is saying, I don't care what duty I do, as long as I'm close. As long as I'm close. *I'd rather be a doorkeeper in the House of the Lord, than dwell in the tent of the wicked, for the Lord is a sun and a shield. The Lord restores favour and honour and no good thing does he withhold from those who walk blameless before Him. Oh Lord Almighty, blessed is the man who trusts in you.*

Folks, it's time to get your yearning for God back. It's time for you to be hungry for God. It's time for you to want Him, to desire Him. Let me show you what I mean. I want you to know, how you can gauge your hunger for God. ***Psalm 42: 1***. *As the deer pants for streams of waters, so my soul pants for you oh God.* One morning as I was praying in the Spirit, I heard these words come out my mouth in English, *'more than ever before, I just need you God. I just need your presence'*. Folks this is time for you to be hungry for intimacy with God again. Just tell Him again, *'I need you God. I can't take another breath. I don't want religion, I just want you. You know, I'm not going to meetings so I can have another meeting, I want you. I'm* *panting, I'm thirsty for you God. Somebody give me Jesus, otherwise all these other extras are not worth it'.*

That's what the deer would do. As it yearns and covets the water, so should you yearn for and covet God's presence. That means, on purpose, seek his face. On purpose tell Him you need Him. On purpose tell Him you can't do anything without Him, even though you've got Him, you need to know His presence like the dew of the morning. On purpose, practice the presence of Jesus, until you form a habit. As you cultivate perpetual time of fellowship with Him, there will be nothing that He will withhold from you, because you are His friend. I'd rather be a doorkeeper in the House of the Lord. My soul thirsts for God.

Let me ask you a question. How thirsty are you for God? Because Jesus said, *blessed are those that hunger and thirst for righteousness*, in ***Matthew 5***, *for they shall be filled*. Also remember the invitation by Jesus, *'Is anyone thirsty*, as He stood up at that great day of the feast in ***John 7*** - *let him come and drink'*. I've never gone up to God and come back disappointed. I've always come back restored, in spirit, soul and body. **Psalm 27: 4** has becomes the desire of my heart. *'One thing I ask of the Lord, this is what I seek, that I may dwell in the House of the Lord all the days of my life'*. David is saying that he wants to practice the presence of Jesus all the days of his life and so do I.

Unlike the Old Testament, where the house was the building, in the New Testament, you are the temple of the living God. *This I seek after - that I may dwell in the house of the Lord forever, just to gaze upon the beauty of the Lord and to seek Him in His temple, for in the day of trouble He will hide me in His pavilion.* This is how you prepare for your day of trouble. By gazing at His face, even when you have good times. You see, most people only go come to church when they're in trouble. But the Psalmists said that it's when you are doing well, that's the best time to gaze at His face. You are preparing yourself so that when your day of trouble comes, He will hide you. I know where I hide in my days of trouble, because I have set the Lord continually before my face.

Psalm 16: 11 says, *'you have made known to me the path of life. In your presence there is fullness of joy and at your right hand are pleasures for evermore'.* ***Psalm 25: 12 - 14*** also says, *'who is the man that fears the Lord? Him shall He teach in the way that he chooses. He shall dwell in prosperity, and his descendants shall inherit the earth. The secret of the Lord is with those who fear Him and He will show them His covenant.'* Did He not say in the book Job that, *'if they obey me, they will spend their days in pleasure.'* There are people who don't like this prosperity message. Well, the whole Bible is a prosperity book. God took people from bondage to give them an inheritance - don't you think they prospered? From building other people's houses to having lands, houses that they did not build, and vineyards they didn't plant, and wells they didn't dig. God has a family and He wants, just like any normal parent, to give them the best He's got. Prosperous in your body, prosperous in your emotions, prosperous in your finances, prosperous in your marriage, prosperous in your mind and every realm of your existence.

Remember, you only become intimate with God if you obey His commandments. The same is true in any kind of relationship. There is no pleasure when there is neither submission nor obedience to each other. Obedience will create intimacy with God. Most Christians are so dry. They feel like God is a million miles away. It does not have to be that way when God has made a way for you. Obedience will create intimacy with God. Remember you are Jesus' friends, His buddies, people He hangs out with, if you keep His commandments.

Obedience is the key to knowing the freshness of God's presence. Obedience will create intimacy. The more intimate with God you become, is the more you will walk in His power and also reflect His awesome attributes and character. If there ever was a time when the people of God needed to radiate the very image of God it is now. The world is tired of seeing Christians who just ware the title but have not fruit to show for the faith that they profess. Gimmicks will not do it; falsehood is easily discerned and religious clichés are ineffective. Only a people that are intimate with God will reflect His nature and person.

Chapter Nine

Evidence Of Love And Honour

One of the most fundamental keys to operating in the *kingdom of God* system is faithfulness. ***Proverbs 28: 20*** says that, *'a faithful man shall abound in blessing, but he who hastens to be rich will not go unpunished.'* The only kind of man that can stay in the continued blessing of God is one that is faithful. Faithfulness is not faithfulness until you have proved faithful. Perpetual obedience is the key to proving faithful. Faithfulness is the principal evidence of your love and honour for God. If faithfulness is the key to the blessing flow, and perpetual obedience is the key to faithfulness, it must go without saying that there can be no blessing and no tangible evidence of love and honour without consistent obedience.

God is the author of life. He is the manufacturer of this machine we call life. Just like any astute manufacturer, God gave the handbook or the manual for operating this machine called life. Therefore, it is unwise for any person to start reinventing the best possible way to live, especially since God's Word has already been tried and tested and it is flawless. Indeed, most of our Christian life is a do-it-yourself job, but there is an instruction manual to go with it. Wisdom will be to save yourself the time and trouble by just operating according the instruction manual, called the Bible.

The issue with God is not how you treat one another. It's not so much your attitude. It's not so much your money - they don't have bank accounts in Heaven. It's not so much whether or not you are trustworthy, or faithful, or dependable and walking in love and meekness. No, all these things are important, but they are secondary. They are by-products of the primary issue. The primary issue is that God has given us His Word concerning all that pertains to life and godliness. Therefore the question is, will you act in line with it? The issue is always obedience.

Obedience demonstrates your love for God. Christianity is not a religion. It is a love relationship between mortal man and an Almighty God. Obedience then, becomes even all the more important because it is the evidence of a person's love for God. To love God is to keep His Commandments. Further more, the evidence of this love will be seen in how you treat other people. The two great commandments are, *'love the Lord your God with all your heart and love your neighbour as much as you love yourself.'* ***Matthew 22: 37 - 40***. In these two, Jesus said, is all the law and prophets fulfilled. However, if you follow it through the New Testament you will find that it zeroes down to how you treat one another. So many folk in the Church are deceived when they claim to love Jesus, and yet cannot stand the people around them. The Apostle John said, 'how can you love God whom you have never seen and yet hate the brother you see?' You're a liar.

When you obey God, you demonstrate that you love Him. Jesus said, if you love me, you will keep my commandments. This is the love of God, that we keep His commandments.

John 14: 31. *'But the world must learn that I love the Father and that I do exactly what my Father has commanded me'*. Jesus said, the only reason the world would know that He loved the Father was because He did what the Father commanded Him. Notice verse 15 also, where He now brings it down to our level. *'If you love me, you will keep my commandments'*. The evidence of your love or the demonstration of your love for God is what you do about what He has commanded you to do. ***1 John 5: 3.*** *'This is the love of God that we should keep His commandments. His commandments are not burdensome'*.

1 John 2: 3 says, *'we know that we have come to know Him if we obey His commandments.'* So people will say, oh, I know God, but they don't obey Him. They don't even know Him. Some of you might actually be strangers to God and for years you thought you knew Him. *'We know that we have come to know Him if we obey His commandments. The man who says, I know Him but does not do what He commands him is a liar'*.

Deception is thinking that you are something that you are not. Everybody can tell you, that's not who you are, but for the life of you, you won't see it and you think the whole world is wrong and you are right. Jesus said that, *'if the light that's in you is darkness, then how great is the darkness?* In other words, if what you believe to be true is a lie, then you are double deceived.

'This is how we know that we are in Him. Whoever claims to live in Him, must walk as Jesus did.' In other words, we must obey God, just like Jesus obeyed the Word.

Obedience will release the perfect love of God in your life. **1 John 4: 16 - 18** says, *'we know and believe the love God has for us. God is love, whoever lives in love lives in God. Now in this way, love is made complete among us so that we will have confidence on the Day of Judgement, because in this world we are like Him, as He is so are we in this world. There is no fear in love, but perfect love drives out fear, because fear has to do with punishment. The one who fears is not made perfect in love.'*

So, He says, if you obey the Word of God, you will be made perfect in the love of God. In other words, the love of God will be complete in you. It will give you confidence. You will always have confidence before God. The reason you have fear, is because you are afraid of punishment. If you want to abide in God, just abide in love. There's no mystery to it. Just love. How do you love? Love is patient, love is kind. It's not rude; it does not keep a record of wrong; It is not self-seeking; it endures all things; Love covers a multitude of sin; it always trusts; Love never fails. Walking in love boils down to practising the above principles. It's that simple. Just ask the questions, Am I rude, am I unkind, am I keeping a record of wrong, am I self-seeking? Am I always wanting to have my way? And am I always failing people? If you can answer those questions, you will know whether or not you are walking in love.

There is no fear in love. I want you to have confidence in the presence of God. You have the blood-bought right to get in the presence of God through the blood of Jesus. Since you have access by the blood of Jesus, when you stand there, I also want you to be confident that the Almighty God, is not going off on holiday, or He's not tired of you praying, or He's not mad with you because you might have not done what He said for you to do. Instead you will have confidence that God will be attentive to the voice of your supplication. This is a covenant promise. God has said that if you keep His Word, He will fulfil His Word on your behalf. He is a rewarder of them that diligently seek Him. I'm expecting my reward every time I obey God. Are you?

That's why it's not okay for God not to do His Word. Why? Because He has already said He will reward you for your obedience. Fear has torment, but you don't have to be afraid, because the love of God will cast out fear. If you obey God's commandments, it is a guarantee that His love will be perfected in your life. Wouldn't it be wonderful with all these things going wrong in the world to be fearless? Just to have an assurance and knowing that, 'a thousand may fall at your side, and ten thousand at your right hand, but it will not come near you. You just watch them fall over. You have no need to be afraid. No plague will come near your dwelling. That's what God's Word does, it gives you information so that you can have revelation knowledge and not be afraid.

Honour, on the other hand, is doing what's right and only because it's right. And the Bible says honour comes from God. The reason people are dishonouring one another in the world, is because honour broke down in the Church. Nowadays we don't even know how to treat one another. We are people of dishonour. Why? Because we didn't honour God first and herefore we dishonoured everybody. I'd rather be honourable by doing what God told me to do. It doesn't matter what you think of me. I don't care. I've got God to please. And the Bible says, *'when a man's ways please the Lord, He even causes his enemies to be at peace with him.'*

Most people worship a god who is a figment of their imagination. One they can tell what to do, when to do it and how to do it. And if it doesn't suit their plans or desires, they endeavour to change the command or simply ignore it. We need to restore God to the place where He belongs. He is an Almighty God, worthy of honour. Just like He said to Joshua in Joshua Five, when the Angel of the Lord showed up and he said, *'are you for us or for our enemies?'* He said, I am not for either. I am not for you and I am not for them. I don't care what you are arguing about, the truth is, I'm for myself and you had better choose which side you are on. However, on the basis of your choice, you are either going to have victories over your enemies, or you will stay bickering for the rest of your life. But the choice is yours.

My prayer is that we, the Church, may rediscover who our God is and also come into an understanding of what gives Him the right and privilege to demand our full obedience. Who is He that He should demand such kind of allegiance and how can we trust him because for years, most of the people that we have allowed to come close to us, or who have had authority in our lives have abused the privilege of our trust.

Obedience is an act of honour to God. And if there is anything honourable about you, obedience will be the evidence of it. God deserves to be obeyed. He is Almighty God. He stands alone in majesty and power. Based on the covenant, however, we can remind Him of His Word to us. But still, it will be along the lines of what He's already told us to tell Him. It's a bloodtight covenant. He deserves to be honoured and obeyed, because He is God.

The question nevertheless still stands. How can you yield yourself and trust someone you have never spent time with? This is a fundamental question that needs to be answered if you are serious about the issue of obedience. The more you spend time with God, is the more you discover how good He is; the more you just let Him be God in your life. This is because you will know, and you would have proved it, you would have tasted and seen that the Lord is good.

Deuteronomy 8: 6 - 7. *'Therefore, you shall keep the commandments of the Lord your God, or you shall observe the commandments of the Lord your God, walking in his ways and revering Him. For the Lord your God is bringing you into a land with streams and pools of water, with things growing in the valley and in the hills. A land with wheat and barley, vines and seed trees, pomegranates, olive oil and honey. A land where bread will not be scarce and you will lack nothing. He's bringing you into a land of abundance. A land where the roads are iron and you will dig copper out of the hills.'*

You see God is always bringing you into something. There is always a greater purpose, place and anointing on the other side of your obedience. **Deuteronomy 6: 23** says that, *'He brought us out from there to bring us into...'* He brought us out from Egypt to bring us into our inheritance. Every time God asks you to obey Him, His intentions are always to bring promotion, wholeness and fullness of destiny to you. God is always going to get things to you, but the condition is, obedience.

Deuteronomy 7: 12. *'If you pay attention, or if you obey these laws and follow them carefully, then the Lord your God will keep his commandments'.* God wants to keep his commandments, if you obey. Now, what does He want to do? Because *He swore to your fathers He will love you, and bless you and increase your number. He will bless the fruits of your womb, the plots of your land, your grain, the new wine and the oil and cubs of your herds and the lambs of your flock, in the land that he swore to your forefathers - you will be blessed more than any other people.*

Christian people have not come into the fullness of their blessing more than any other people. But I announce to you that it is possible that the covenant of God should produce not only the wealthiest men, but the most soundly made people, health wise, mental wise, physically, spiritually, socially and financially if they obey God. The scripture teaches that to the faithful, God will show Himself faithful. In other words, God is obligated by your acts of honour, which are evidenced by your obedience, to do the honourable thing in your life. What is the honourable thing? It is to keep His Word concerning every area of your life. Therefore, before we concluded that certain things will never work in our lives, maybe we need to ask the question, 'have we been honourable towards God by walking in obedience towards Him?

It is an honourable thing to obey God because your obedience always has repercussions on other people. You will either lock other people up, or release them by you obedience. Based on whether or not you obey, some people might come into a blessing or a curse. So, it is selfish when we just think, oh well, nobody else is affected if I disobey God. The truth is, there is always somebody else who is affected. Every time you obey or disobey God, somebody else either gains or loses out.

The most sobering example of this principle is found in the book of ***Romans 5: 17 - 19.*** This is the example of Adam and Jesus. *'For if by the trespass of one man death reigned through that one man, how much more will those who receive God's abundant provision of grace and of the gift of righteousness reign in life through the one man, Jesus Christ. Consequently, just as the result of one trespass was condemnation for all men. So, also the result of one act of righteousness was justification that brings life to all men.'* [So one offence - all punished. One act of righteousness - all acquitted]. And then he says, *'for just as through the disobedience of one man, many were made sinners, so also through the obedience of one man, many will be made righteous.'.*

What an awesome principle. Just because Jesus got it right, if you believe in Him, God sees you righteous. Just because you chose not to carry on what your fathers did, your family has broken the generational curse. One act of righteousness can mean blessings for all. If you have no reason to obey God, do it for the sake of your children. Obey God for the sake of your loved ones. Just obey God because many people will be blessed or not blessed, based on your actions. Your obedience will lock or release somebody else.

For instance, when you got born again, think about how many of your family members were subsequently saved, because one day you said, I repent. Then think about all those that have come to know Jesus because of you. Heaven will be really fascinating. Just because you gave someone a lift and they came to the meeting and they got born again. And then all their family got delivered from all kind of bondages and now they are all serving God. They have led a thousand to Christ in their lifetime, and then God says, all that's in your account. All you did was just give one person a lift to a Church meeting.

No wonder Solomon admonishes us saying, *'whatsoever you find to do, in the book of Ecclesiastes, do it with all your might'*. You are a trigger for someone else's miracle and breakthrough.. You have got a specific purpose. That's why I don't care what kind of hell the devil throws at me. You have to determine to obey God regardless. Set your mind and make the decision that you are going to do the will of God. Even if it costs you more than you thought you could afford; you and I are the triggers that are to be pulled and released in order for others to get their victory.

Chapter Ten

My Personal Journey Of Obedience

This chapter has been inspired by the advice of my wife, Linda, who wanted me to add a personal touch to this book. Here I share some of my own personal experiences in life where, obedience has been the key to my journey. It is always somewhat difficult for one to talk about oneself, mainly because of the risk of being misunderstood or even suggesting that they have done everything right. Nevertheless my prayer is that as I share some of my own personal struggles and successes, God will use them to inspire hope and courage for those of you who are having to make tough choices in order to obey God.

I was born in Zambia in a city called Kitwe on the Copperbelt province. I am the fourth child in a family of nine children. For as long as I can remember, I have always known that I was born for a specific assignment, which would take both discipline and focus in order for it to be accomplished. I remember the first verse of the Bible that my mother taught me to memorise at the age of 3. To this day, this scripture is one of the pillars of my life and ministry.

Psalm 1: 1 - 3 says, *'blessed is the man who walks not in the counsel of the ungodly, nor stands in the path of sinners nor sits in the seat of the scornful, but his delight is in the law of the Lord and in His law he meditates day and night. He shall be like a tree planted by the rivers of water, that brings forth fruit in its season, whose leaf also shall not wither and whatsoever he does prospers.'*

I can remember determining in my heart, as little as I was while I stood in front of the whole church reciting that verse, saying I am going to be that blessed man. I determined that I should not endeavour to build my life any other way but by the counsel of the Lord. Looking back now, I really did not have the intellectual capability to be making such decisions, but the same Holy Ghost who works in the adults was the same Holy Ghost that was at work in me. Consequently, until the age of ten, I always felt like most of my peers' interests were somewhat shallow, and of no real appeal to me at all. From then on almost all my close friends have been at least five years older than me. With the help of diligent parents, who taught us the Word of God every night before we went to bed, I found myself so hungry for the things of God so much so that my Sunday School teacher asked my to help her teach one of the classes. I also loved to worship God and I was also asked to lead our local Church in praise and worship from when I was about twelve years old.

Since I was younger, it seemed to me that God had blessed me with two things. A likeable personality and a spirit of positive expectation in life. You know, I just love people and I think that people are the greatest comedy show that ever happened. Consequently, I was always making fun and joking about the many idiosyncrasies that different individuals have. However, there were many times when I was faced with the real choice between having fun and doing something that I believed would contribute to my assignment in life. I sacrificed many football games, which was my second passion in life. But having parents that loved me, and still love me, unconditionally was the greatest key to knowing how to obey those in authority without any sense of inferiority or fear of them abusing that privileged position. I learnt what a wonderful thing it is to yield to those who are over you in authority and are determined to do you good regardless of what you do or don't do.

Sadly, having been brought up in Church all my life to this point, I was always wondering what it was like to not be a Christian. The main thing that prompted such a curiosity was the hypocrisy and carnality that I saw among Church folk. As a matter of fact, most of my non-Christian friends treated me better than the born-again, water-baptised, tongue-talking folk that went to Church all the time. Consequently, during my early teens, I rebelled against God because I hadn't matured in wisdom and understanding to distinguish between what was man's doing and what was the Lord's. Knowing the kind of parents that I had, I did not publicly profess not to love God because I had too much honour and respect for them. So for nearly eighteen months I had backslidden. Thank God for His grace that appeared to me and rescued me from my foolishness and all that the devil had led me into. I realised that sin was not as good as the assignment for which I was born. I thank God for His willingness to speak and get through to me in the midst of all my confusion.

Having been restored to fellowship with God, I was now dealing with the fact that I had to break up my relationship with my non-Christian girl friend because what fellowship would light have with darkness. One the qualities that I have always treasured is that I am an all or nothing kind of person. Therefore, when I came back to God, I gave Him my all and I have never looked back since. The biggest challenge, though, became that of renewing my mind from all the junk that I had allowed to come in during my backslidden state. The more I worked on renewing my mind by the Word of God, the easier I found it to obey God's will for my life. To this day, one the biggest disciplines of my life is that of constantly renewing my mind. That is because renewing your mind is not an event; it is a process.

Anyway, as I grew older and left school, I felt that God was saying to me that I should leave the town where I was born and go Lusaka, where God said He would position me for what He was going to do next in my life. I can remember sharing this with both my parents and my Pastors, and how I was not sure whether or not they would believe that God had spoken to me. Suffice it to say that they both reluctantly released me to obey God. Even so, it was still a frightening thing to do for a sixteen-year-old boy. Now I look back and realise it did not make sense for even my parents to release me at all. But I thank God for their sensitivity to the voice of God and also for believing in me enough to respect the that fact I had heard from God to move to a city that was two hundred miles away from home. At every point of moving to the next level in my life, God has always asked me to obey Him by following a specific course of action. I am also so grateful that He has always made His Word Good to me.

I arrived in Lusaka looking for work with no experience at all. The closest place I could find a place to stay was about thirty miles away from the city. God has always been faithful even in times of transition. He has sometimes, almost at it were, put me in temporary positions while He is rearranging things for my maximum blessing. I have therefore learned not to despise the day of small beginnings because I know that whatever God said, if I obey Him, it will come to pass. An opportunity came up for an Accounts Clerk job in a chain of stores in Lusaka and I was offered the job. I had been working at this firm for about eight months when one morning I realised that the owners were into idolatry because I found them performing their rituals and sacrifices in the office building. My spirit was very troubled and as I prayed, I felt God say to me that I should resign that same day, which I did.

At this point I was working on getting a place at the university of Zambia to further my education. However, the following day my father rang me from Kitwe saying that He was driving up to Lusaka in a few days time to pick up some friends of His from England. When my father came to Lusaka, instead of picking me up after he had dropped these friends at the hotel, he felt prompted by the Lord to come and pick me up first. As we drove from the airport, these friends of my father started asking what I was doing with my life. So I told them I was actively seeking to get into university and I had just resigned from my job the same week. One of them said I know that Bradford College are giving scholarship to international students. Just leave it with me. Time elapsed and I started working in a Commercial Bank. Unexpectedly, I received a letter from these friends of my father saying that I had been given a scholarship to pursue studies at Bradford College. I now look back and see how even though my obedience to God cost me a job because of making a stand for righteousness, that God had better plans for me. God will never ask you and me to do something that is to our disadvantage.

Anyway, I arrived in England with only twenty pounds to my name because all the money that I had saved went to supplement the amounts that someone gave my father for my air-ticket. Needless to say that I went through four years of studying without owing any one anything even though my scholarship only covered my tuition fees. God provided more than £42,000 for all my rent, books, subsistence and all. To this day I could not tell how He did it but I know that He did keep His Word.

During my first year at College, they put me on an initial two-year course that was supposed to bridge the gap in order for me to be admitted onto the degree programme. While I was praying one day, God said to me you could do this course in one year instead. So I went and said this to my personal tutor. His response was that no one in the history of the school of business at the college had ever done that before. After much deliberation, they agreed to let me attend both year one and year two classes. They said, if within 3 months my performance did not come up to the standard of the average second year student, they would not allow me to continue. God was faithful and He fast tracked me, finishing the course with distinctions all around. Again obedience saved me a year's worth of work. God will always supply the ability for you to do what He has asked you to do.

During my stay in Bradford, I met a beautiful young lady by the name of Linda Vine. We got on so well but the only problem was that she was English. This was a problem because it had the potential to mess up my plans of going back to Zambia as soon as I graduated. I therefore argued with God about this because by now I knew that He had called me into the ministry and the person who I married was definitely going to be a big part of this assignment. Again I had to yield my will to God's will and today, I cannot imagine not having Linda as my wife. She is indeed a help mete, by my side.

While we were engaged to be married, we started pastoring a group of people, about 35 adults and some children. Shortly after we were married, Linda felt that God wanted her to leave her job and start her own business. After praying about it we both agreed that she would leave at Christmas. Meanwhile, I was now working for another company as a Business Development Manager. Toward the latter end of September I was offered a promotion. This would have meant leaving the Church with no one to look after it, because our leadership team was still just in its early days. Anyway, the choice for my job came down to moving or being made redundant. Our Church was not in any position to support any full time staff at all.

Linda and I believed that we were, and still are, in the centre of God's will for our lives and so leaving town was not an option. Further, starting her own business was the only option for her, because we believed it was the will of God for us. Again, the test of obedience was the key. I went and resigned and Linda did not withdraw her notice of resignation either. We were both potentially unemployed but we didn't care because we knew we were in the perfect will of God for our lives.

The same week that I resigned, God spoke to me to move the church, which had grown to about fifty people, into the city centre. I was praying and I heard the Spirit of God say to me from ***Revelation 3: 7***, saying *He had set before me an open door and no man can close it. He said that even though my strength may be small He would uphold me.* Financially, we were broke and did not have the money to negotiate a lease nor did we have the money for chairs and other essential things. After sharing this with the Church, within the seven days, that followed, God provided the finance for us to pay for the first three months on the lease of a 16,000sq feet building and also enough to purchase two hundred brand new chairs.

On making the move into the city centre, the membership of the church practically quadrupled within six months. By this time I had also started pastoring the Church on a full time basis and now we have 6 staff members and growing. Linda also started her new business, which we called, *'The blessing'*, and in the first year of trading, her income almost tripled. The power contained in God's Word is released when you choose to take Him at His Word. Two years have now come and gone and we are still going from strength to strength.

One of the major keys to releasing me into my destiny and assignment has been the people that God has strategically equipped and sent across my path. These people have come with practical help, insight, wisdom and admonition. The strange thing, though, has been the fact that the trigger to finding such people has only occurred after the exchange of obedience. I honour and cherish all those wonderful people that God has graciously used in my life so far, because they too have had to obey God in order to act with favour towards me. When you obey God, you do not have to worry about who doesn't like you or who is not making room for you. I have proved over the years that promotion and favour only come from the Lord. The Bible says that, *'even the heart of the king is in the Lord's hand, and He turns it whichever way He pleases.'* If you continue to obey God, He will make sure that you do not serve before obscure men because God has a wonderful tendency of making room for those who honour Him by their obedience.

When God spoke to us about pastoring our Church, He told us to gather His people around the Word. The instructions were for us to gather together and hear the Word preached under the anointing so that faith may come for any situation in life. Everybody in the Church was to sit under the same Word. As the Church started growing, I begun to feel under pressure from people whose primary reason for attending Church was social interaction. There were also people from other Churches who were disturbing our members saying, your Pastor preaches too much and it was not healthy for their growth. Consequently, we took the decision that we would put everybody into small groups. I had clearly allowed our leadership team to disobey God's Word to us. From the day we announced this decision, everything started going wrong. The peace in the Church was disturbed, the anointing on me was not as strong, the finances begun to diminish and we all seemed to lose the sparkle. Clearly, we were conforming to the pattern of how we had seen other Churches organised but the truth was, it was not the will of God for us.

As the spiritual head of the house, I called an extra-ordinary leadership meeting after four weeks of this going on. I first of all repented before God in their presence and then also asked for their forgiveness. It turned out that everyone on the team could sense from the day we took the decision to break the Church into smaller groups that we had missed our assignment. Therefore we all went before God in repentance. I was supposed to be ministering at another Church the following Sunday morning but I cancelled the engagement because I needed to lead my team into corporate repentance before God's people. Sunday morning came and I stood up and did the same things that I did with the leadership team. I apologised to the whole Church for having diverted from our assignment. You see you have to be more desperate for God's approval than you are to keep your ego and save your face. Today the Church is going from strength to strength because of our obedience. By the way, there is nothing wrong with small groups if that is what God has spoken to you about.

After about 3 months into Restoration House, our new premises, God spoke to me again concerning publishing the Word of Faith that we preach on every available voice. He said for us to launch ***'Get Understanding Television.'*** In the first place, we did not know anything about television and secondly, we did not have the finances that such an endeavour demands. I shared this with our leaders and we started to negotiate contracts with some broadcast companies. One day just after the meeting, a man came up to me and said that God had told him to come and give me a cheque for us to purchase a television camera. It was a large sum of money and we knew again that God's hand was on this part of our ministry. Today Get Understanding Television is broadcast three times a week all across Europe, and once a week in parts of the North America and Zambia. I believe that the full story is yet to be written. But if God did it for me, Linda and the Centre Of Life Church International, He can and He will do it for you because He is no respecter of persons. However, the key to all this has been obedience. Timely obedience and sometimes going against all rational and intellectual reasoning is the master-key to unlocking your assignment in this life. Whatever, He tells you to do, just do it!! Remember, wisdom is the principal thing; therefore get wisdom and in all your getting, get understanding.

Pastor Ramson B. Mumba Jr. has an extensive Bible teaching ministry, which reaches as many as 60 different countries on the three continents of Europe, North America and Africa through broadcasts. We have therefore just included a selection of some of the best-selling titles from the several teaching series that he has done in recent years.

To order your copies or to join our Tape Series of the Month Club, or receive a free colour brochure, please contact us at the following address;

Centre Of Life Church International

Restoration House

Nelson Street

Bradford, BD5 0HD

West Yorkshire, England

Tel. +44 (0) 1274 724557

Fax. +44 (0) 1274 742523

Website: www.centreoflife.org

Email: information @centreoflife.org.

The Power Of Simple Obedience

Walking In Manifested Revelation

Don't Perish, Get Your Revelation

The Spirit Of Wisdom And Revelation

The 5 Characteristics Of Divine Revelation

Walking In Manifested Revelation

Increasing Your Measure Of Faith

What To Do When It Is Not Working

Making The World Of Hope A Reality

Discerning Your Present Level Of Faith

How To Increase Your Measure Of Faith

Righteousness, Peace And Joy

The Kingdom Of God Is Righteousness

The Covenant Of Peace

Joy Unspeakable

Taking Hold Of Your Destiny

Taking Hold Of 'That' - 1

Taking Hold Of 'That' - 2

Unlocking Your Uncultivated Potential

Manifesting The Word Of God

The Power Of The Abiding Word

Releasing The Rhema Word

Transformed By The Abiding Word

Immeasurably More By The Word

Understanding The Laws Of Abundance

God's Obligation To The Righteous

The Righteous Prosper In God

The Cost Of Abundant Peace And Prosperity

Faith - The Title Deed Of All Abundance

Faith, Fear, Doubt And Unbelief

Faith, Fear, Doubt And Unbelief

Don't Raise My Hope

Walking In The Fullness Of The Anointing

Burden Removing, Yoke Destroying Power

The Message Of The Anointed And His Anointing

The Purpose And Effects Of The Anointing

Walking In Fresh Anointing Without Hindrances

The Reality Of Righteousness

The Reality Of Righteousness

Walking In The Reality Of Righteousness

Becoming A 100Fold Return Person

God Is Not A Respecter Of Persons

Understanding - The Master Key To Self-defence

Preparing For Your Day Of Trouble

Mastering The Spirit Of Offence And Strife

Antidotes To Worry

'Hearing And Doing' - The Key To A 100Fold Return

The Anointing To Pastor
The Anointing To Pastor
How To Release The Anointing

The Covenant Of Peace And Exchange
The Covenant Of Peace And Exchange
The Covenant Of Exchange
The Law Of Release And Exchange
The Law Of Ability And Exchange

God's Way Of Healing That Works Every Time
God's Plan Of Wholeness For Mankind
Healing And Salvation Are Both Parts Of Redemption
Taking Hold Of Your Covenant Of Healing
By His Stripes You Were Healed
God's Way Of Healing That Works Every Time

How To Overcome Impossibilities
How To Overcome Impossibilities
Impossibilities And Faith That's Turned Loose
Impossibilities And The Anointing Factor

God's Willingness To Heal
God's Willingness To Heal
Sickness Is Not Good News, Healing Is

How To Cultivate A Sound Mind

The Anatomy Of Man

The Mind - The Bridge To Abundant Life

The Thought Process And Mental Turmoil

How To Tame Your Thoughts

Thought Prescription For A Sound Mind

How To Manifest The Will Of God For Your Life

Bringing Good From The Good Treasure

Becoming The Good Word Stored In Your Heart

How To Manifest Good And Perfect Gifts

Your Future Is Released By Your Words

The Word Is Near Your Even In Your Mouth

The World, The Religious And The Word System

The Three Distinct Life Systems

Hallmarks Of The World System

God's Way Of Doing Things

Keys That trigger Restoration

Prophesy Life To The Dry Bones

Time To Pursue, Overtake and Recover All

Praise Your Way Out Of Trouble

If You Can See It, You Can Receive It

Recovering Your Lost Hope

Born Into A Living Hope

Recovering Your Lost Hope

Arise And Shine

The Year Of The Glory Of God

The Year Of The Overflow And Plenty

Arise And Shine For Your Light Has Come

Manifesting The Glory By The Anointing

Restoration Of God's Glory Brings Wholeness

How To Overcome Temptation

Recognising Moments Of Temptation

Kinds Of Temptations And The Faithfulness Of God

How To Overcome Temptation

The Power Of Simple Obedience - Volume 1

The Power Of Simple Obedience

Obedience And The Goodness Of God

Obedience - A Question Of Trust

The Power Of Simple Obedience - Volume 2

Ten Reasons Why We Should Obey God - 1.

Ten Reasons Why We Should Obey God - 2.

Ten Reasons Why We Should Obey God - 3.

Ten Reasons Why We Should Obey God - 4.

Ten Reasons Why We Should Obey God - 5.

Ten Reasons Why We Should Obey God - 6.

How To Manifest The Presence Of God

How To Manifest The Presence Of God

The Abiding Presence Of God

How To Release The Ability Of God In Your Life
The Power Of Delighting Yourself In The Lord
Operating In The Rhema Word
Releasing The Spirit Of Faith

The Making Of A Leader
Discovering Your Gift And Being Faithful To It
Developing Integrity And Skilful Hands
Renewing Your Mind For Leadership
The Difference Between A Dream And A Vision

Unlocking Your Covenant Of Prosperity - Volume 1
God Takes Pleasure In Your Prosperity
Money With A Mission
The Anointing To Prosper
How To Connect To The Anointing
Divine Exchange Through Seedtime And Harvest

Unlocking Your Covenant Of Prosperity - Volume 2
Introducing El Shaddai & Jehovah
Passing The Prosperity Tests
Understanding The Four Ways Of Giving
The Blessing of Melchizedek & El Elyon

Help! I am Going Through The Storm
Mastering The Storms Of Life
Preparing For Your Day Of trouble

How To Get From The Problem To The Answer
Developing An Inner Image Of The Covenant
Your Company Determines Your Perspective
Meditation-The Key To An Inner Image - 1
Meditation-The Key To An Inner Image - 2
How To Meditate On The Word Of God

Faith - The Established Lifestyle For The Righteous
The Just Shall Live By faith
Understanding The Law Of Faith
Believing With The Heart
Believing With Unshakable Confidence
We Believe And Therefore We Speak

Where There Is No Vision The People Perish
Defining The Purpose Of Vision
Vision Is Opportunity In Present Circumstances
God's Vision Is A Global Vision
The Power Of Biblical Partnership
Receiving The Prophet's Reward

Unveiling The End-Time Glorious Church
God's Estimation Of The Church
The Glory Of The Latter House
Founded On The Anointed And His Anointing
Manifested Love - The Principle Distinction

Principles Of God-Centred Praise And Worship

A Portrait Of The God We Serve

Spirit And Truth - Keys To Sound Worship

Worship Is Having A God-Centred Lifestyle

Putting On The Garment Of Praise

How To Overcome The Spirit Of Division

How To Overcome The Spirit Of Division

One Lord, One Faith, One Baptism, One Body

How To Overcome The Spirit Of Offence

How To Overcome The Spirit Of strife

Envy And Competitive Jealousy

The Vain Glory Trap

How To Overcome The Spirit Of Unforgiveness

Embracing The Ministry Of Rcconciliation

The Covenant Of Wholeness

The Covenant Of Wholeness

The Ministry Of Angels In The Covenant

Developing Greater Faith In The Covenant

The Anointing Of Wholeness By The Word

From Brokenness To Restoration Of wholeness

God's Will For You Is Wholeness

Methibosheth Should Have Been King, But

Keys To The God-Kind Of Wholeness

Come Out And Stir Yourself Up

The Power Of Simple Obedience

How To Be Led By The Spirit

God's Way Of Communicating With Man

How To Recognise The Voice Of God

The Counsel Of Trusted Friends

Led By Your Peace And Understanding

Led By Your Conscience And Gifts Of The Spirit

The Word - God's Most Sure Way Of Leading You

Get Understanding Celebration - Volume 1

Discovering Your Gift And Being faithful To It

Developing Integrity And Skilful Hands

Restoration Of God's Glory Brings Wholeness

Developing An Inner Image Of The Covenant

Get Understanding Celebration - Volume 2

Renewing Your Mind For Leadership

The Difference Between A Dream And A Vision

The Just Shall Live By Faith

Understanding The Law Of Faith

Get Understanding Celebration - Volume 3

The Anointing Of Increase And Overflow

How To Overcome The Spirit Of Division

Decision - The Key To Releasing Destiny

Sickness Is Taken From The Midst Of Us

How To Lay Hold Of Your Inheritance

How To Become A Christian

If you would like to accept Jesus as your Lord and Saviour, pray the following prayer;

Heavenly Father, thank you for sending Jesus to die on the cross for me. I believe with my heart that you raised Him from the dead and with my mouth I confess Jesus as my Lord and Saviour. I repent of all my sins and I thank you that you have forgiven my sins. From this day forward, I will live for you and fulfil the purpose for which I was created. Thank you for giving me a fresh start in Jesus' name.
Amen.

If you prayed the above prayer, please contact us and we will send you some information to help you in you new found way of life. God bless you richly.

Ramson.